MW00683163

The Journal

The Helter Skelter Rock 'n' Roll quarterly

Issue #1
Summer 2001

Helter Skelter Publishing

The Journal

The Helter Skelter Rock 'n' Roll quarterly

Editor: Peter Doggett

Published by Helter Skelter Publishing
4 Denmark Street, London WC2H 8LL

ISBN: 1-900924-38-2

Subscriptions and advertising will be available with future editions.

All correspondence, including books for review, should be addressed to the editor at the above address.

Submissions are welcome for future editions.
Please send sae or irc's for return of typescript.

For editorial comments or queries, contact doggett@dircon.co.uk
For all other enquiries about Helter Skelter, contact
helter@skelter.demon.co.uk

Designed by Caroline Walker

CONTENTS

The Cast

DEBBIE CASSELL is a singer-songwriter whose superb debut album, *Angel In Labour*, was critically acclaimed by *Mojo* and *Q*, and almost immediately went out of print. For more information on how to obtain a copy, e-mail debbiec@dircon.co.uk

PETER DOGGETT is the author of *Are You Ready For The Country* (a new paperback edition was published in late spring) and the former editor of *Record Collector* magazine.

JOHN ROBERTSON is a Beatles expert whose books include *The Art And Music Of John Lennon* and the somewhat shorter *Lennon*.

JOHNNY ROGAN is perhaps Britain's most renowned rock biographer, whose subjects include Morrissey & Marr, the Byrds, Van Morrison, the Kinks, George Michael and, most recently, Neil Young.

A Few Words From the Editor

WHILE THE circulations and fortunes of most British rock magazines have been in free-fall for the past year, the market for books about every aspect of rock and pop culture has never been more buoyant, or more eclectic. Yet aside from an occasional review in the broadsheets, or a book-of-the-month splash in *Mojo* or *Uncut*, few rock books receive anything more than 100-word reviews in the monthly mags – small reward for projects which can require years of dedicated research, and which can often transform the way that we hear the music we love.

Hence this journal, which aims to provide more detailed and incisive coverage of the best and most significant rock literature of recent months, and to trace some of the themes and ideas which have inspired these books and their authors. It is also intended for debate, even argument. This first, experimental issue was written and produced by a small band, but we're open to intelligent, witty and forthright comments and contributions from anyone who shares our slightly scary passion for rock literature.

YOU DON'T KNOW ME:
THE LIMITS OF BIOGRAPHY

by Peter Doggett

THE PUBLICATION over the last year of weighty hardback volumes about two of rock's most enduring icons, Bob Dylan and Neil Young, has set high standards for their rivals to match. Two of these biographers, Clinton Heylin and Johnny Rogan, were expanding and extending the scope of books which were produced during their respective apprenticeships as professional writers – Heylin's previous edition appeared in 1991, Rogan's as long ago as 1982. Although Heylin's volume retains the core of his previous work (adding some 50% more text, and revising much more than that), Rogan's book is an entire fresh affair, more than three times the length of his initial Young biography (*Neil Young: Here We Are In The Years*).

More recently, Howard Sounes has unveiled a rival account of Dylan's life to Heylin's, pinning the promotion of his book on an apparent revelation about the singer's second marriage. (See the appendix to this piece for more discussion of Dylan's numerically vague family.) *Down The Highway: The Life Of Bob Dylan* (Doubleday, £17.99) occupies the same space on the shelf as Heylin's revamped text, although closer inspection reveals that Sounes's book is barely half the length of its competitor.

Despite being beaten into the shops by a full year, Sounes spares little praise for Heylin, or indeed his predecessors: "While good work has been done, the challenge of writing a major biography that conveys the full grandeur of Bob Dylan's artistic achievement, and also reveals the true life of this fascinating and elusive man, has remained." Yet his own text separates life and art in a fashion which eludes any hint of grandeur. Sounes's prose is flat to the point of lifelessness, and is never sparked into passion by Dylan's music. His critical insight rarely extends beyond the bland platitudes contained in his preface: "He is a great recording star … On stage, he is truly dynamic … Dylan has become more than an entertainer. He is a minstrel guru to millions who hear their deepest thoughts and feelings expressed in his songs." While Dylan's first biographer, Anthony Scaduto (*Bob Dylan*, 1971), was able to describe his songs with such vividness that they took on three-dimensional shape, Sounes never excites the reader to rethink or revisit Dylan's music. By his own standards, his book automatically fails one of his key tests for "a major biography".

His success regarding his second requirement, "the true life", is more ambiguous. Sounes isn't inspired by context, and all too often Dylan moves through his text like an actor who has stumbled in front of a cartoon backdrop. To select one example at random: Sounes notes the release of Dylan's 'George Jackson' single in 1971, but doesn't attempt to grapple with its confused political message, its awkward reception by the rock community, or its significance as the singer's first overt piece of 'protest' for many years.

Certain personal dramas also escape his grasp. Spectators of Dylan's erratic live performances in the early 1990s were enmeshed in a psychological and physical decay which seemed destined to end in tragedy. But aside from Dylan's wilfully unsettling appearance at the 1991 Grammy Awards, Sounes refrains from comment on this nightly soap opera.

Yet *Down The Highway* certainly isn't bereft of impressions of Dylan's "true life". The great strength of the book is the doggedness of Sounes's research: foremost among his coups, as already mentioned, is his confirmation of Dylan's 'secret' marriage to Carolyn Dennis. Remembering his training as a tabloid journalist, he has leaned heavily on primary sources: "Nearly everyone of significance in Dylan's life was contacted and new interviews were conducted with most of these people." Among the names in his list of interviewees were several which raised the temperature of Dylanologists – Dylan's sometime lover Carole Childs, his childhood friend Larry Kegan, his ex-manager's widow Sally Grossman and (most revealing of all) his Woodstock neighbour in the mid-to-late 1960s, Bruce Dorfman. This last witness supplies the most compelling testimony of the entire book, unearthing the seeds of Dylan's interest in painting and adding significantly to our understanding of this enigmatic period.

Down The Highway is studded with such anecdotal gems, ensuring that even the most jaded Dylanologist can draw sustenance from unexpected novelties. And for the general reader, Sounes's account may provide the most accessible entry available into the misty maze of Dylan's life and times. Yet there is little in his book to inspire such a novice to investigate the art which is surely our only excuse for raking through the debris of his subject's life. And Sounes is unable to weave his undoubtedly attractive fragments into a tapestry that explains or in any way contains his mercurial quarry.

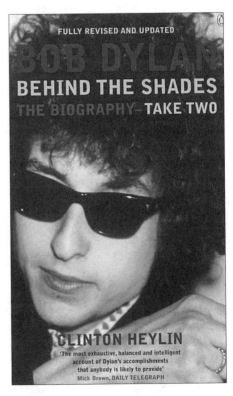

THE VERY title of Clinton Heylin's *Bob Dylan Behind The Shades: The Biography, Take Two* (Viking, £20) promises more substance: both an investigation of the man behind the persona, and a reappraisal of the author's original analysis. Those themes are duly extended in his preface, which also raises some fundamental questions about the nature of his project.

Even in his first edition, Heylin was aware of the limitations of the biographer's art. "A credible biography is a bringing together of strands," he wrote in his preface. "It draws from all and distills down to a point of view. With a living artist the picture can never be complete. This book can only be a signpost along the way." A decade later, his perception hasn't altered: "I am still writing about a moving target".

But elsewhere in his twin prefaces, Heylin charts an important shift of focus. In 1990, he was avowedly searching for traces of Dylan's work in his life outside art. Now, he notes, "I presume to document a constant, unresolvable conflict between man and artist".

He is steered towards this course by a quote from Dylan's former guitar technician, Cesar Diaz, who provides a devastating analysis of his employer, which shadows the 600+ pages to follow. Debunking the popular view of Dylan as a confessional artist and emotionally committed performer, Diaz says: "I think the greatest masterpiece he has ever pulled off is the fact that he can make people believe that part of him is involved in the writing of those songs. To me each song is a play, a script, and he'll be that guy from the song for that moment, but [then] he'll change back to Bob ...But he actually convinces you that yes, it is me who is talking to you and I'm being sincere about it."

Heylin notes intelligently that Diaz's perspective is that of a man who worked with Dylan only between 1988 and 1993; but this almost heretical judgement reverberates through the rest of the book, rattling our secure notions of who, and what, Bob Dylan is supposed to be.

Equally forbidding is the closing paragraph of Heylin's new preface, in which he effectively closes the door on his subject as a functioning artist: "The burden of being Bob Dylan has broken more than the man's back. The dissolution of his worldview, his romantic attachments to women unworthy of the moniker Muse, the failure of artistic resolve brought on by his chronic indiscipline, and a frustrating disregard for extracting the most from that dying voice within, makes for a quite different portrait from that of the fifty-year-old Dylan." Small wonder that some of Dylan's more entrenched followers have greeted Heylin's biography as an artistic assassination attempt.

Yet the great strength of *Bob Dylan Behind The Shades* is its author's willingness to encompass both glory and disaster in Dylan's life and work. If he is necessarily dismissive of Dylan's more erratic adventures since 1985, he is equally open to, and awestruck by, the indescribable majesty of his finest work (in this instance, 'A Hard Rain's A-Gonna Fall'): "How a twenty-one-year-old Dylan encapsulated the magic and mystery of a five-hundred-year-old ballad, the deep dark truths of Dante, and the apocalyptic symbolism of the French poets and the beats into six and a half minutes of sheer terror ...can never be realized by cold literary analysis, the tautologies of historical incidence, or even by mere biography." This strikes a note of humility which has not always been found elsewhere in Heylin's work, but which is apparent on occasions in *Behind The*

Shades. Nothing in Sounes echoes Heylin's awe, or the perspicacity of his artistic judgement.

Heylin's account of the gradual transformation of Hibbing teenager Robert Zimmerman into the arrogant folk poet Bob Dylan is compelling, masterfully weaving together succinct critical analysis, solid research and telling anecdotes. The pace never slackens through Dylan's reincarnation as a rock'n'roll star, his Woodstock retreat, and his creative and public re-emergence in the mid-70s.

Yet the impact of his detailed, yet propulsive narrative is not to separate the man from the artist, as he suggests in his preface, but to merge them into one. Even when Dylan himself claims to be distanced from the cast of 1974's 'Lily, Rosemary And The Jack Of Hearts', apparently supporting Heylin's quest, his boast is undercut by the evidence of the art – and, in what is perhaps the finest chapter of the book, the testimony of Dylan's muse for the *Blood On The Tracks* album, Ellen Bernstein. Her valuable insight into what may be the artist's finest work is supported by Heylin's exclusive access to Dylan's notebook covering the genesis of the record.

Throughout the book, Heylin relies heavily on the engaging and authoritative voices of those who knew and (in some cases) loved Dylan. To their contributions he adds his own impeccable research, and brief but intelligently opinionated critiques of the artist's work, which are slightly sardonic, unpretentious, but convincing.

Yet there are boundaries to his knowledge – or, at least, his ability to communicate it. Obvious constraints (i.e. the threat of arousing libel lawyers) may have restricted Heylin's account of Dylan's erratic behaviour and apparent ill health in both the late 80s and the early 90s. Similar discretion seems to have been applied to his family life (see the appendix below). The unwillingness of those who are still Dylan's close associates to betray his confidence cuts off another means of access to his recent activities.

The result is that after 1982, Heylin's narrative loses some of its multidimensional force, and settles into a more familiar history of Dylan's career – still intriguing and entertaining, but not as compelling as the coverage of the man's first 40 years. There are exceptions to this rule – the soap opera of Dylan's involvement with one of his sidekicks and her girlfriend, for instance, and Heylin's harrowing glimpse of Dylan being consumed by "the Darkness" at the start of the 90s. But the Dylan of today somehow eludes his biographer – perhaps, Heylin seems to suggest, because he is also eluding himself.

In a judgemental but also chilling conclusion, Heylin parades a line of women whom he condemns as inappropriate muses for Dylan in middle-age; and then returns to the harsh verdict of his introduction, portraying Dylan's recent worldview as dark, negative and alienated. Though the book ends on a note of comparative optimism, that note is overwhelmed by an anecdote about the burden of fame from Dylan's friend David Amram. Standing outside a crowded bar, Dylan stares gloomily within, and informs Amram: "I don't know what kind of a scene it is, but after I've been there it's gonna change." And it does. Hence, no doubt, the shades which Clinton Heylin, despite his valiant efforts, never quite removes.

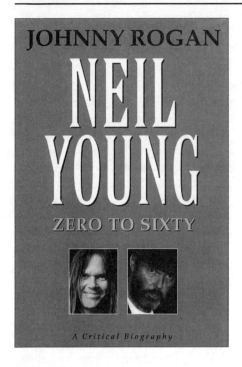

THE TITLE of Johnny Rogan's *Neil Young: Zero To Sixty – A Critical Biography* reverses the title of Young's song, 'Sixty To Zero', and has led at least one innocent commentator to assume that the singer has recently reached his 60th birthday (which actually falls in November 2005).

Playfulness aside, Rogan offers no clues to his choice of biographical approach in his disarmingly brief, and – on the surface, at least, almost irrelevant – introduction.

While Heylin lays out his theoretical principles from the start, Rogan is more reticent. He begins with a pen-portrait of his subject: "Neil Young has always been engagingly modest about his achievements. A legendary contrary figure, he has at times dismissed the past and rubbished his own albums with a grin on his face." Then he reminds the reader of his pedigree as a biographer: "Scholarship, criticism

and reportage are three different skills which I've always attempted to bring together in writing books on popular music". And finally, in his only overt statement of intent, he explains: "With Neil Young, the emphasis is more solidly on the work than any of my previous books – thus the subtitle: 'A Critical Biography'."

Just when you might expect Rogan to propound his critical principles, and to suggest themes and theories against which he will be judging Young's work, he veers instead into a lengthy, and (superficially, at least) absurdly self-indulgent paragraph which reads like a missive to his therapist, or at best a flagrant piece of self-mythology: "Someone once said that I was obsessed with the past …I spend an inordinate amount of time mulling over past events …usually in search of some Holy Grail perspective that is unattainable …Focusing on the past has its own advantages. Part of the subconscious process in writing books of this nature is the need to confront the past anew and see things from a wiser, more reflective perspective, while hunting for a happier or at least more convincing ending. If only life could be so obliging – and maybe sometimes it is."

Rogan is too intelligent a writer to have inserted this paragraph merely as a piece of compulsive autobiography; and sure enough, some 650 pages later, the book ends with his subject also being forced to confront his former self: "Throughout his life, Young has been running away from immersion in the past …Recently, though, his past – that great enemy to all his future endeavours – has finally threatened to upstage his present."

The reference is to the bulky archive projects – audio and video anthologies, CD box sets and the like – which have interrupted Young's progress for more than a decade. "Now, it seems," Rogan suggests, "the enveloping archive is systematically draining his output and threatening to overwhelm him by its sheer volume …The terrible paradox he faces is the constant need for renewal while knowing that each new project will delay the completion of the archive, which now looms large as the final creative ambition of his life."

It's an arresting notion, which (like Heylin's judgement of Dylan) casts a fresh, if dark, light on Young's recent career. But then Rogan offers an uncharacteristically tame and evasive ending: "The archive release will happen when Young is ready and with luck its completion may inspire some adventurous new work. Where all this will leave Young's reputation is a question that will probably still be debated long after his death." The reader of a self-professed *Critical Biography* might reasonably think that the debate should already have begun here.

Without an over-arching discussion of Young's stature as an artist, and his importance within the rock canon, Rogan's *Critical Biography* is left to rely on its song-by-song, album-by-album analysis. At its worst, these comments are strictly pedestrian: almost every song, no matter how banal, receives its due descriptive paragraph of description, and at times the author retreats to précis rather than criticism. Rogan also appears more comfortable with words than music, which means that he sometimes neglects to note the melodic similarity between Young's songs ("War Song" and "Ocean Girl" are a pair that spring immediately to mind).

These occasional lapses are all the more surprising in the vicinity of Rogan's dis-

cussion of Young's masterpieces, such as *On The Beach* and *Sleeps With Angels*. In particular, his five-page analysis of 'Ambulance Blues' is as perceptive, and insightful, as any rock criticism I've ever read. His comments that the *On The Beach* songs "expose (Young's) shortcomings unmercifully …the results are particularly revealing and gain added force as a final condemnation of his former self" open the door to a fresh interpretation of Young's deepest work.

Even more effective is Rogan's analysis of the puzzling (and mostly unregarded) *Sleeps With Angels* album, which is preceded by the author's minute awareness of Young's shifting relationship with his God. (Other reviewers have noted with amusement or revulsion Rogan's distaste for Sinéad O'Connor's assault on a picture of the Pope, and his comments on abortion; equally telling about the author's beliefs is his comment that the song 'Star Of Bethlehem' is "as shocking in its insouciant agnosticism as the heretical 'Soldier'".) Yet Rogan moves beyond imposing his own moral code on Young and to the reader to chart the full cosmological implications of a record that even the most informed critics have previously heard as nothing deeper than a response to the death of Kurt Cobain. At full stretch, the author has no peers in his chosen field.

Nor should the *Critical Biography* tag be taken as an admission that Rogan is light on original research into Young's life. On the contrary, like Heylin he has travelled far and wide to unearth previously unheard witnesses, whose testimony is particularly valuable in those areas which have been explored in least detail elsewhere. Mid-60s folkie Vicky Taylor, for instance, provides often hilarious commentary on Young's own folk years, and his early romantic entanglements. Rogan himself adds a suggestive comment about Young as folk troubadour, one which has resonances for the rest of his career: "Like the classic method actor, Young found it difficult to distinguish between the mask and the man ...while he performed (folk) music he played the part and was no less sincere than the other youngsters who carried acoustic guitars and spoke of the politics of peace."

The balanced elegance and dry humour of Rogan's prose is particularly noticeable when he introduces his interviewees, creating sharp, three-dimensional portraits of key figures.

The book is equally effective over longer distances, such as the Springfield's final year, which Rogan paints as a time of growing but divergent ambitions, moral expediency, human drama, and lost opportunities. There's a compelling account of the fiasco surrounding Young's signing to Geffen Records in the early 80s, and the legal aftermath; and just as Heylin can excite fans with the revelation that, yes, there really was a Mr. Tambourine Man, Rogan unveils titbits about the exact complexion of the lost *Homegrown* album, and the merits of previously undocumented 70s songs such as 'Florida' and 'Mexico'.

Bizarrely, Rogan's blend of critique and biography begins to lose some of its force at exactly the same chronological moment as Heylin's, for similar if not identical reasons. Unlike Dylan, Young has, as far as we can ascertain, been happily and quite privately married for two decades. Aside from his responses to his son Ben's serious illness, we know virtually nothing about his personal life during this period. So, like Heylin, Rogan is forced back onto events –

and (*Sleeps With Angels* aside) his account of the last decade is a mere parade of fanzine facts: tours, guest appearances, charity benefits and albums. Though Rogan admits that this has hardly been the most creative period of his subject's life, he holds back from Heylinesque attempts to explain why that might be, beyond his comments on the psychological weight of the *Archives*.

LIKE DYLAN, then, Young eventually evades being captured by his most serious biographer, blocking his pursuer's progress with the distractions of his artistic career. Yet the ultimate inability of both writers to subdue their subjects, in the manner of those Victorian naturalists who pinned butterflies to a page, hints at the difficulties involved in creating a definitive portrait of a living person – particularly when the subject has not allowed access to his archives, or offered fresh interview material.

In creating 'unofficial' versions of their characters' lives, both Heylin and Rogan are necessarily disarmed by the discretion of friends and associates, by the lingering shadow of the libel lawyers, and by the knowledge that future events might place the past in an entirely different perspective.

Heylin's reliance on interpreting the testimony of his witnesses, and Rogan's attempt to explain the man through his work, are equally admirable and offer compelling entertainment. Yet the gaps in their knowledge – and their insight – leave their subjects free to wriggle from their grasp, aware that although these two authors have cut closer to 'the truth' than any of their predecessors, a sense of mystery still remains. Ironically, by refusing to theorise about his subject's life or work, Howard Sounes is able to provide an account which, on the surface at least, appears more definitive than Heylin's or Rogan's. Yet his 'success' has to be balanced against the dramatically reduced ambition of his project, in which the mere collection of anecdotal evidence is its own reward.

On some levels, death can be said to liberate the biographer. In his twin account of Tim and Jeff Buckley (*Dream Brother*; 4th Estate, £17.99), for instance, David Browne can claim to provide judgement on his deceased heroes, who are not able to prove him wrong. He is also freed from legal concerns in his discussion of father and son's bad habits; the same stories that

appal your press agent when you're alive only enhance your legend once you've passed beyond the rescue of your learned friends.

But as the long-running disputes about the accuracy of Albert Goldman's portrayals of the posthumous Elvis Presley and John Lennon have shown, even death cannot deliver something as complex as a human being into the hands of his Boswell. The art of the biographer – and, for that matter, the autobiographer as well – is to deliver a fictional re-enactment of real life that has the taste and smell of truth. And the limit of biography is that fiction, no matter how intelligent or well researched, is perhaps all it can ever hope to deliver.

CODA: BOB DYLAN'S HAPPY FAMILIES

"Get a bunch of kids who call me Pa
That must be what it's all about"
(Bob Dylan, 'Sign On The Window')

BIRTHS, DEATHS, marriages: a reader can be excused for assuming that such vital statistics are the foundations of biography. Not in the view of Clinton Heylin, who admits: "Knowing of at least one of Dylan's children by one of his eighties backing singers back in 1991, I nevertheless chose to respect their right to privacy. I decided that it had no obvious bearing on the relationship between the man and his art – unlike, that is, his relationship with the lady in question – and would unnecessarily draw the man's ire."

His morality may be admirable, but the prurient, curious and factual-minded among us might be disappointed by his reserve. There were no such checks in the mind of Howard Sounes, who achieved international publicity for his Dylan biography by revealing that the singer married Carolyn Dennis, after she had given birth to their child, Desiree Gabrielle Dennis-Dylan, in January 1986. As the Dylan magazine *Isis* perceptively noted in a review of Sounes's book, the use of nursery rhymes as the basis for many of the songs on the 1990 album *Under The Red Sky* may have been influenced by bio-graphical as well as artistic impulses.

Not that Heylin ignores the birth of Desiree Gabrielle, even if he doesn't print her name. Writing about the 1986 tour, he notes: "Gospel singer Carolyn Dennis, having ...returned to his affections, was again with child, about to make Dylan a father for the sixth or seventh time." (The relevance of the word "again" in that sentence is not revealed.)

Heylin also quotes a book proposal by another of Dylan's former lovers, Susan Ross, which claimed that the musician had had three wives and eight children. And he refers to an intriguing interview Dylan gave to Charles Kaiser of the *Boston Review* in 1985. Asked whether he had remarried after his divorce from his first wife, Sara, Dylan apparently replied: "Yes, in a manner of speaking. Yes, as a matter of fact." When? "About '80." And was he still married? "I'm not sure." Heylin reports that in January 1980, Dylan was reliably reported to have purchased an engagement ring; that year he also wrote and performed a song entitled 'The Groom's Still Waiting For The Altar'.

Heylin skirts around the precise details of Dylan's 'secret marriages' in the 1980s; Sounes states baldly that Dennis was his second and, to date, last wife, and makes no reference to the Kaiser interview. A humble critic might note these biographical discrepancies, and venture a far-fetched theory of his own: perhaps the marriage Dylan referred to in 1985 was not physical but spiritual? Maybe he saw himself as a Bridegroom of Christ, baptized into a state of union which only his own apostasy could sunder? But of course that wouldn't excite the supermarket tabloids…

Then there are the children. Sounes has the birthdates, Heylin is altogether more imprecise. First, there was Maria (born October 1961), Sara's child from before she met Dylan. Heylin says that Dylan's son Jesse was "well on the way" when Bob and Sara married in November 1965; Sounes dates the birthdate as January 1966. Both sources agree that Anna was born in summer 1967; and that's three (Dylan had officially adopted Maria as his own).

Sounes confidently announces that a fourth child, Samuel, was born in July 1968. Heylin notes Samuel's bar mitzvah in 1982, but strangely surrounds his birth in a layer of mystery, describing Dylan returning home to Woodstock in summer 1968, "seemingly to witness the birth of another son. A photo by Elliott Landy taken in Woodstock in the fall of 1968 appears to include this son, held firmly in Sara's arms, Maria, Jesse and Anna at her feet. However, no such son was cited in the 1977 divorce proceedings, nor is there any record of him being bar mitzvahed." There are two immediate explanations for this apparently fractured logic: either Heylin has simply become confused, or else he is hinting that there is some unstated complication about Samuel's parentage.

Additional chaos is added to the family saga when Heylin talks about Sara's youngest son, Jakob, being due in spring 1971; Sounes dates his birthday as being 9th December 1969. Given that, in an interview with *Rolling Stone* in 1997, Jakob said, "I'm 27 years old", Sounes appears to be correct.

But Heylin introduces an intriguing theory of his own when he notes that Dylan's 1985 book *Lyrics* was "dedicated to his newborn daughter Narette". Sadly, this is his only mention of the child in his entire 375,000-word text. Meanwhile, Sounes says that there is "no evidence" that Dylan has had any children apart from the five from his marriage to Sara, and one by Carolyn Dennis. All of which leaves one marriage, and one or two children, unaccounted for, if Susan Ross is to be believed. Never mind the groom: the biographers are still waiting at the altar.

ALAN McGEE & THE CREATION MYTH

by Peter Doggett

IN THE book of Genesis can be found two conflicting versions of the creation myth. The first is short, dramatic, and focuses solely on the Begetter of All Things. The second is longer, fraught with conflict, and finds the Great Helmsman ceding centre-stage to his flawed creations.

In an uncanny parody of scripture, the demise of Creation Records has been documented by two rival chroniclers, whose divergent techniques mirror the dichotomy of the Old Testament. The first account to be published was *Alan McGee & The Story Of Creation Records* by Paolo Hewitt. As the official biographer of Creation's last major discovery, Oasis, he had already secured his place within the label's inner sanctum, and had befriended its founder, Alan McGee.

Comprised entirely of verbatim interviews, complete with hesitations, repetitions and interruptions for his subjects to answer their mobiles, Hewitt's book portrays Creation's history as a cartoon cocktail of daring, drugs and rock'n'roll. (No one has ever accused Creation of selling sex.) As one of McGee's closest associates told me, "It's a real rock'n'roll book. It's like the MC5 – dangerous and loud."

The book's first interviewee is Hewitt himself, who explains to Creation veteran Ed Ball how he was approached with the idea by a publisher, and how he then sought McGee's approval: "I tell him I was offered a book on him. He says do it. But there's another book being done, I say." McGee bats the objection aside, and invites Hewitt round for a three-hour interview, in which he seduces his prospective biographer with tales of cocaine debauchery, theatrical anger and nervous collapse.

In avowed search of "the overall

picture", Hewitt takes the strange decision to ignore Creation's artists and concentrate solely on McGee's backroom staff. But his narrow scope allows him to revive the 'great man' theory of history, in which a single figure controls not just his own destiny but the fortunes of a culture. Even at his most unscrupulous and ramshackle, McGee emerges from Hewitt's pulp nonfiction as a Malcolm McLaren for the post-punk generation, an inspired maverick who will let nothing short of life-threatening excess distract him from his anarchic vision of rock'n'roll mayhem.

The rival Creation saga could not be more different in scope or style. While Hewitt's book bears all the signs of an official imprimatur from its subject – McGee even writes a self-serving foreword – David Cavanagh's *My Magpie Eyes Are Hungry For The Prize: The Creation Records Story* presents itself as an epic of objective historicism, displayed across a vast canvas that comprises the rise and fall of British 'indie' culture over the last two decades. Yet there are clues in his own introduction that Cavanagh too began his project (which takes its title from a lyric by 80s Creation band, the Loft) with an inside track to the heart of McGee's empire. He describes his "marathon series of interviews" with the Creation boss, and includes within his list of acknowledgements virtually the entire cast of Hewitt's book, plus literally hundreds more – Creation artists, their managers, disaffected former staff, heads of rival labels, journalists, PR analysts; anyone, in fact, who can provide perspective on McGee and his rise to the summit of the independent record industry.

Between the motion and the act, the

THE CREATION RECORDS STORY
My Magpie Eyes are Hungry for the Prize

David Cavanagh

shadowy McGee seems to have cannily switched his loyalty from the steely-eyed historian to the affable insider. As Hewitt tells Ed Ball, "I don't know if McGee is a publicity junkie who loves the idea of having two books on him, or if he genuinely felt that the other book would be so detailed it would miss the point." The accusation that Cavanagh's book had sacrificed analysis for detail, losing the dramatic thrust in the minutiae of record releases and shifts of office personnel, has been repeated since by McGee's cabal – and, most damningly, by McGee himself, who effectively poured scorn over Cavanagh's efforts in *The Guardian*.

Yet for anyone beyond McGee's immediate orbit, his dismissal of Cavanagh's work seems not merely unjust, but positively perverse. Where Hewitt maintains a steady lens on McGee as the personification of rock'n'roll rebellion, Cavanagh expertly controls an enormous cast of characters, slowly and tellingly narrowing the focus onto McGee and Creation as they emerge from the debris of the 80s indie scene to achieve worldwide success with Oasis. Hewitt paints Alan McGee's success as a triumph of willpower, one individual beating the odds; Cavanagh offers a more complex tale in which Creation remains little more than an extravagant sideshow, until two accidental happenings – the merging of rock and acid house, and the discovery of Oasis – propel the label into the limelight.

At odds between the two versions is not just a portrait of McGee – Hewitt's machiavellian general and instinctive genius against Cavanagh's entrepreneurial gambler. More revealing is the gulf between their attitude towards Creation's ethos – one book assuming the innate importance of McGee's every manoeuvre, the other implicitly challenging the basis of his reputation. Beyond that, where Hewitt revels in extravagant gestures, Cavanagh sees a less immediate but ultimately more significant drama: the tortuous attempts of the British rock underground to retain its precious independence against the twin enemies of corporate ambitions and public apathy. It's that struggle which lends Cavanagh's book its narrative tension – and which overshadows Creation's rise and fall.

THE INDIE ETHIC

As a regular contributor to British rock magazines over the last decade, Cavanagh has a sharp eye for the debasement of the indie ideal. "The original meaning of indie", he writes, "described a culture of independence that was almost a form of protest; a means of recording and releasing

music that had nothing to do with the major labels." In the early 21st century, by contrast, indie is all about "bands that play guitars and don't sound like Britney Spears".

At the heart of indie culture is one aim, to control one's own destiny; and one fear, of 'selling out'. Within that framework, there has been a 20-year debate about the precise definition of 'indie', particularly in relation to the prestigious national independent sales chart. Cavanagh documents the gradual blurring of the battle-lines, as labels such as Some Bizzare and Kitchenware accept a degree of corporate distribution, but retain power over their output and financing. By the end of the 80s, political integrity has begun to weaken beneath the assault of dance music, which threatens to overwhelm the white boys' rock club. By the time that the mighty Sony Corporation buys 49% of Creation's shares in 1993, there is apparently little innocence left to lose.

No enterprise epitomised the indie ideal better than Rough Trade, spearheaded by Geoff Travis (whom Cavanagh describes as "a colossus"). He summarises his manifesto: "We wanted to deal with music whose reason to exist was nothing to do with its commerciality. All that mattered was whether or not the record gave you a thrill." That credo was originally shared by Alan McGee, a Scottish teenage outsider who found a context for his ill-defined alienation in the cauldron of punk. Yet as McGee tells Cavanagh, his immersion in the music business, first as a performer (with the Laughing Apple) and then as the creator of an indie label, always had a wider agenda: "I was ambitious. I wanted to be successful. And Rough Trade was the only part of the music that would let me in."

The swaying fortunes of Rough Trade, and its role as Creation's distributor during the 80s, occupy much space in Cavanagh's book; one of its great strengths, in fact, is that it lends drama to previously under-valued aspects of the record-making process. Early in the labels' relationship, the nature of compromise becomes a live issue, as Travis secures Rough Trade's future by agreeing to collaborate with Warner Brothers on a "indie front-of-house" imprint called Blanco Y Negro. One of the new concern's first signings is a band of Scottish punk terrorists called the Jesus And Mary Chain.

The group had debuted on Creation with the feedback-laden 'Upside Down', and aroused such a media frenzy that McGee agreed to manage them. Two years into his career, he had to decide whether to let his most visible signing join a major label subsidiary. "They wanted a living in music and I couldn't give it to them," he tells Hewitt. "I thought I could probably make another 10 or 15 Creation records from the money that we made out of managing the Mary Chain. So that's why I did it."

The Mary Chain's success lent Creation a frisson of danger which rapidly entranced the British music weeklies. "I found when I joined *NME*," Hewitt remarks sardonically, "that all those writers hated the fact that they missed punk, and they were always trying to relive it." Though the group soon sacked McGee as their manager, he was able to mastermind a Warners liaison of his own, the short-lived Elevation label.

By 1987, as Cavanagh reports, McGee's self-image was ballooning. Though Creation had yet to release anything approaching a hit record, its boss was boasting that "I really do believe that right now it's Creation – including Elevation – against the whole business." With the Mary Chain gone, he threw the label's thin financial resources behind the House Of Love, whom he characteristically claimed as the greatest band in the world. The painful story of their brief brush with success, and subsequent fall from grace, dominates the central section of Cavanagh's book, illustrating the band's idealism and hubris in equal proportions. The House Of Love live out every flickering fantasy of rock'n'roll stardom, and emerge exhausted and empty, all their major league pretensions reduced to a flimsy bluster.

Their long decline mirrors Cavanagh's portrait of the disintegration of the indie scene during the late 80s. He quotes Iain McNay, the former head of another indie label, Cherry Red, to devastating effect: "The word 'indie' had become a marketing word that ...had absolutely nothing to do with either the original intention of the chart or even the meaning of the word."

Alan McGee was about to experience all the implications of that contradiction. While Creation's fortunes were buoyed at the start of the 90s by Primal Scream's unlikely transformation from Stooges-obsessed rockers into indie dance icons, any financial gain was swiftly consumed by less productive areas of the label's roster – notably My Bloody Valentine, whose laudable attempts to deconstruct rock history threatened to have a similar impact on the indie market.

With his flagship now shipping dangerous quantities of water, McGee began to search for a saviour with a big bucket. He signed a US deal with the little-noticed SBK corporation; sent his fellow executive Derek Green off to discuss a UK buy-out by the indie/major fencesitter, China

Records; and then promptly sold almost half of Creation's stock to Sony, allowing them the option to return for the rest in another four years.

Cavanagh rightly treats this as a pivotal moment, and he highlights the way in which McGee masked the full extent of the Sony deal from the indie-fixated UK weekly press, and also the reaction of a purist fan who spat at the Creation boss in disgust at his apostasy. Hewitt, by contrast, chooses not to question whether McGee suffered any qualms about his decision, as if he assumes the subject will automatically be taboo.

The two books are equally polarised when Oasis enter the story – and McGee allows them to sign to Sony worldwide, with Creation as their UK licensee. Once again, the British press weren't informed; and predictably Hewitt lets the matter alone. Anyway, such delicacies were soon lost in the hubbub of 'Britpop', as Oasis topped the British album charts with their debut, and then released the most successful UK record of the era, *What's The Story (Morning Glory)*.

Creation rapidly became an emblem of British industry at its most inventive, although press officer Andy Saunders tells Cavanagh: "There wasn't a label identity as much any more, because it was all geared towards making Oasis a success. Any kind of indie philosophy …had gone out of the window." And he accuses McGee of failing to notice that the label had fallen prey to "a corporate virus" that "changed the whole vibe of Creation completely".

In 1996, McGee was confronted by a corporate spectre that he couldn't ignore, as Sony returned to claim the remaining 51% of Creation shares. He successfully

acted the wounded innocent in the *NME*, threatening to resign if Sony's scavenging wolves had their way, almost as if he'd never seen the Faustian contract he'd signed with the major four years earlier.

Yet at the height of Creation's cultural power, McGee finally seemed to notice that the label had strayed far from its original spirit. With even indie-inclined employees like Andy Saunders stating that the tag was now "a bit of a swear-word to us …it denotes underachievement", there was little to connect the plump Creation of the late 90s with its 80s skeleton. Only the often flamboyant folly of some of McGee's signings – Mishka, Kevin Rowland – was a reminder of the company's origins. In October 1999, McGee prepared plans for the label to be dissolved, telling Cavanagh that "by being with Sony, we're becoming a fucking dinosaur".

While Hewitt's coverage of this era merely echoes McGee's own pronouncements, Cavanagh suggests (but never quite lays out) a more cynical interpretation of the Creation supremo's rediscovered idealism. Throughout his lengthy book, he highlights the way in which McGee's definition of success edges ever closer to the mainstream. Like Peter Mandelson and his Labour Party project, McGee seems to assume that maintaining the company brand will conceal, or at least excuse, a multitude of compromises.

That comparison is stated openly to Cavanagh by Creation marketing director Tim Abbot: "The brand equity of Old Creation was about having no profit ethic; it was lunacy and mis-matches and experiences second to none. New Creation was, to me, 80s yuppie materialism. It had no emotional spirit. It wasn't driven by art." Mandelson would have smiled at Abbot's bare-faced realism, though this master of political manipulation would have baulked at leaving his tracks so plainly in the sand.

In his guise of maverick business guru, a Richard Branson for the indie era, McGee found himself being stalked in the mid-90s for endorsements and contributions by Mandelson's devilish creation: Tony Blair's Labour Party. McGee was now describing himself as a "capitalist with a conscience", and for almost a year either side of the 1997 election, he became Blair's pet bulldog, lending (to mix yet another metaphor) his aroma of rock'n'roll outrage to Labour's bland brew. Hewitt reports him lambasting "people like Tony Wilson … who are just corporate whores now sucking up to the music industry". But maybe he had by now removed all the mirrors from his own office.

In October 1999, McGee renewed his independent credentials, telling Cavanagh: "I would now argue that whoever you go into bed with, you ultimately – unfortunately – start to look like them." He then dissolved Creation, and formed the determinedly cultish Poptones label, which he describes as "totally anti-establishment, anti-music business, totally left-field … I might never have another hit record in my life". And who funds this exercise in the indie ethic? Venture capitalists from the City of London. Even Cavanagh is too polite to point out the full implications of McGee's logic.

CHANCE AND CHAOS: THE THREE COUPS OF ALAN McGEE

In both accounts of Creation's history, three events dominate the horizon, fuelling the label's myth and also ensuring its continued existence at moments of financial distress.

(1) THE JESUS AND MARY CHAIN

"If it hadn't been for the dynamism of Alan's own personality, Creation would have been treated as a joke", Fire Records boss Clive Solomon tells Cavanagh about the label's early months. What transformed Creation's standing was the explosive arrival of the Jesus And Mary Chain, whose confrontational music and chaotic concerts inspired adulatory hype from the UK music press.

Yet, as Cavanagh notes, the band's ferocious sound owed less to inspired planning than to incompetence: "Thanks to a combination of a recalcitrant PA, a lot of alcohol and their own inexperience, the Jesus And Mary Chain had made the most astonishing music McGee had ever heard." But Cavanagh also credits McGee with realising the power of what fate had flung in his path: "The Jesus And Mary Chain had found the one man on the London scene who hated and loved pop music as much as they did, in the same measures and for the same reasons. The one man, too, who ran his record company on principles of aggression and brinkmanship, and who hoped some day to take his vendetta to the highest towers of the music business."

(2) PRIMAL SCREAM

Creation's leather-wrapped rock warriors were marooned by public disinterest when acid house DJ Andrew Weatherall remixed one of their ballads. The result was 1990's 'Loaded', the commercial highpoint of the marriage between rock and house, which in turn spawned *Screamadelica*, Creation's biggest-selling and most influential album up to that point.

As both Creation historians reveal, Alan McGee's involvement in this coup (facilitated by the Scream's Andrew Innes) was minimal. "Alan McGee never got house music," the label's former PR man Jeff Barrett pointedly tells Cavanagh. "Alan McGee got ecstasy."

For once, Hewitt includes an anecdote that is even more dismissive of McGee's reaction. "What no one ever mentions is that McGee turned the idea down," says Barrett's partner in Heavenly Records, Martin Kelly. "I was there when Jeff rang him and asked for some money to put Weatherall in the studio. McGee said, 'Barrett, you're bonkers, they're a rock band'."

C) OASIS

McGee rightly sees no shame in admitting that his discovery of Oasis in an almost deserted Glasgow club was "a complete fluke", an accident of time and place transfigured by a magical vision of potential glory.

More intriguing is another, more painful coincidence, which snatched McGee from the frontline just as his new signings were being introduced to the world. In February 1994, he suffered a particularly disturbing nervous collapse in Los Angeles, was briefly hospitalised, and spent the next year recuperating. The following month, Oasis's debut single was released.

In McGee's absence, and to his subsequent amazement, Creation then set up its first marketing department – and Oasis were guided to national and then global fame, with only the most minimal of input from their mentor. Hewitt includes a poignant quote from McGee, in which he admits that he felt distanced from their success, and had virtually no influence on their music after their first album. It's the ultimate irony: the events which propel McGee to the forefront of the UK music industry take place while he is effectively removed from the fray. Even for a man who had happily accepted chance and chaos, this must have seemed one accident too ambivalent to relish.

WE THINK SO YOU DON'T HAVE TO ...
CRITICS AND THEIR CHOICES

by Peter Doggett

MORE THAN 1,000 albums are released every month in Britain alone. Record stores today carry a wider selection of music, in everdtttty imaginable genre, than at any time in the past.

Never has a reliable roadmap to this bewildering musical landscape been more necessary. Hence the proliferation in recent years of listener's companions – the All-Music Guides and Music Hound volumes from America, the Rough Guides from Britain, and many more of their kind, broad and narrow, fallible and reliable.

The quest to guide the public towards the promise of quality has inspired four markedly different books in recent months. They vary in intelligence and intention, breadth and approach, and their critical criteria range from numerical popularity to blatant subjectivity. "Never trust the artist, trust the tale", wrote D.H. Lawrence. But can you trust the critic to advise you which tale to trust?

200,000 MUSIC FANS CAN'T BE WRONG

Colin Larkin is the author of the book, but *All-Time Top 1000 Albums* (Virgin, £16.99) is based upon "over 200,000 votes from fans, experts and the critics". While critics and experts are left to debate the precise differences between their rival camps (Do experts not criticise? Are critics not expert?), fans can luxuriate in what's claimed as "The world's most authoritative guide to the perfect record collection".

Leaving aside all discussion about whether democracy is the ideal method to determine any kind of perfection, Larkin presents the people's choice in strict order of popularity, although there are no hints about exactly how many people preferred No. 562 in his list (Phil Collins' *Hello, I Must Be Going*) to No. 563 (Little Feat's *Dixie Chicken*). Nor does he explain whether the votes of the critics and experts were weighted against those of the general public (some of whom might rate their opinion above those of a hundred self-righteous journalists).

Accompanying each album is a paragraph of explanatory prose, sometimes naive (as when Larkin describes Portishead as "scruffy but brainy", with the tone of a teacher guiding a maverick pupil towards his GCSEs), sometimes insightful, but utterly lacking in any kind of pomposity. He's an enthusiastic amateur, not a self-ordained guru, and his remit allows him to do no more than disagree gently with his voters' tastes. "On songs like 'Think Twice', she milks each note for all it's worth," he complains mildly about

Celine Dion's *The Colour Of My Love* (No. 856 in his list). "And when I say milk, I mean milk." Or, you might think, something even more tasteless than that.

Much newspaper debate was prompted by Larkin's Top 5, which suggested that Radiohead now rival the Beatles as the most important band in rock history. (In another decade, that verdict will either seem ridiculously presumptuous, or timidly conservative. My money's on the former.)

More surprising is the statistical breakdown of his survey: in the eyes of his votes, the 90s is now the favoured decade for modern popular music, followed by the 70s, the 80s and, almost as an afterthought, the 60s. Norman Tebbit must be delighted.

Refuge in such numerical analysis is inevitable as you consult the plethora of appendices and tables which surround Larkin's main listing. His 1,000 albums include 49 soul albums, more than 50 jazz, but just 10 blues (only five of them by black artists), 19 country (only one by a 'traditional' performer, *Johnny Cash At Folsom Prison*) and 16 reggae (nine of which feature Bob Marley). There are 14 records apiece by the Beatles and Miles Davis, 13 by Bob Dylan, 12 by R.E.M. and 11 by the Rolling Stones; but none by Muddy Waters, Willie Nelson, Tony Bennett or Funkadelic.

As compensation for the necessarily mainstream content of his book, Larkin endearingly offers personal selections of his favourite singles, albums that he considers lost gems (by mostly late 60s and early 70s artists as recherché as Starry Eyed And Laughing and Rhinoceros), and 50 recommended jazz albums. This last listing is intended for someone "who has discovered *Kind Of Blue* and wants to find

out more, but is so intimidated by jazz that he or she does not know where to go. Having experienced this painful transition, I know how it feels." And some readers may indeed prefer to throw themselves into the arms of one paternalistic critic than those of 200,000 fans.

THE GOSPEL ACCORDING TO MOJO

Like Larkin's collaborative volume, *The Mojo Collection* (edited by Jim Irvin; Mojo Books, £14.99) offers a vast selection of recommended albums, with explanatory text – puffed as "The Ultimate Music Companion", no less. This weighty volume shares none of the glossy elegance of its parent magazine, looking more like a railway timetable (remember the days when the trains ran to time?) than an invitation to a musical feast. Equally anonymous are the identically professional texts, which provide 300-to-750 words of reliably informed *Mojo*-style context for each record, usually with exclusive quotes from the artists or their entourage; but which lack the sense of individuality that would have been supplied by including the authors' names.

No fewer than 75 journalists and associates of the *Mojo* empire selected and annotated this impressive collection of short essays, which run in strict chronological order, and make no attempt to evaluate Miles Davis against Jimi Hendrix, or Travis against Frank Sinatra. With one glaring exception (*Mojo* found the only critic in the world who rates Paul McCartney's *Wings Wild Life* album), the contents represent either a predictable cross-section of critical consensus, or a *Mojo*-tinged voyage into the obscure (with space for cult names like Sun Ra, Shirley Collins and Ted Hawkins).

While popular appeal pulled artists like the Backstreet Boys into Larkin's orbit, *Mojo*'s team prefer a slightly more predictable selection of pundits' favourites from recent years: please welcome Flaming Lips, Beck and Bonnie 'Prince' Billy.

Missing from this galaxy are several of the titles which featured in the Top 50 of Larkin's poll – U2's *The Unforgettable Fire*, for instance, the Beatles' *Rubber Soul*, Pink Floyd's *Wish You Were Here*, the Rolling Stones' *Let It Bleed* and R.E.M.'s *Out Of Time*. Strict rationing – only the Beatles are allotted more than five titles, a peak reached by Bob Dylan, Frank Sinatra and Neil Young – ensures that *The Mojo Collection* surfs hundreds rather than dozens of names. Even then, the omissions may be covered by the additional sections on reggae, soundtracks, lounge music, and compilations. (Other apparent omissions are explained by the vagaries of the index, which lists, for instance, Van Morrison under 'V'.)

The churlish might complain that the world music selections owe more to the vogueish tastes of rock fans than to musical or cultural impact (Os Mutantes and the Buena Vista Social Club are in, but there's no room for Caetano Veloso or Om Khalsoum). The committed might query the inclusion of, say, Bob Dylan's *Time Out Of Mind* at the expense of *John Wesley Harding*, or the omission of all but the first Velvet Underground album. And the broad-minded will note that, once again, country music receives short shrift: there's an album each from Willie Nelson (his standards collection, *Stardust*) Merle Haggard and Hank Williams, but nothing from Emmylou Harris, Waylon Jennings, George Jones, Dolly Parton, Randy Travis, Lefty Frizzell, Tammy Wynette, Bill Monroe or indeed any traditional bluegrass artist. Even in the cosmopolitan whole-world view of *Mojo*, it seems, some music seems destined to remain forbidden.

DON'T MESS WITH THE DEAN

American rock saboteur Richard Meltzer published a superb collection of his lifetime's work last year (*A Whore Just Like The Rest*, published by Da Capo; its title merely hints at its author's emotional dislocation from the mainstream of rock criticism). This vast array of essays and reviews included several random assaults on the reputation and person of his one-time editor at *The Village Voice* in New York, Robert Christgau.

"Did I tell you that Christgau, good old Bob, once dubbed himself The Dean of American Rock Critics?", Meltzer writes in an essay entitled 'Vinyl Reckoning'. (Newcomers to his prose should note that fantasy and reality are often indecipherable outside their immediate context.) He continues in outraged tones: "He had a T-shirt made up with his name above that title, and a likeness of Little Richard …The Dean to this day (in his syndicated 'Consumer Guide') gives LETTER GRADES to albums and has a routine enabling him to monitor, or simulate monitoring, the complete 'curriculum' – every current release."

The T-shirt may not exist, and the title of Dean was probably awarded rather than self-appointed, but Christgau's 'Consumer Guide' survives within the pages of the *Voice*, and since 1969 he has been allotting grades (from A+ to a rarely sighted E-) to new or recent releases across the popular spectrum – with priority given to what Christgau dubs "semi-popular music" (alias cult or genre favourites).

While Meltzer might not be alone in questioning the value of rating records as if they were school projects, Christgau's reviews are masterpieces of concision, erudition, insight and humour. At their best, his pithy, questioning, exploratory prose can illuminate – or devastate – a career within a single sentence. More often, each review – often no more than 100 words long – is an exquisitely balanced blend of wisdom, fierce opinion, and street smarts. And Christgau is a savage destroyer of illusions, as valuable in identifying the faults of a critically-lauded record as he is in unearthing an obscure rave of his own. Here, in full, is his response to Radiohead's *OK Computer* (the second best album of all time according to Larkin's book):

"My favorite Pink Floyd album has always been *Wish You Were Here*, and you know why? It has soul, that's why – it's Roger Waters's lament for Syd, not my idea of a tragic hero but as long as he's Roger's that doesn't matter. Radiohead wouldn't know a tragic hero if they were cramming for their A levels, and their idea of soul is Bono, who they imitate further at the risk of looking even more ridiculous than they already do. So instead they pickle Thom Yorke's vocals in enough electronic marginal distinction to feed a coal town for a month. Their art-rock has much better sound effects than the Floyd snoozefest *Dark Side Of The Moon*. But it's less sweeping and just as arid."

Christgau's Consumer Guide: Albums Of The 90s (St. Martin's Griffin, £16.99) is his third collection of reviews. Whereas his 70s guide was rooted firmly in the mainstream, the 80s volume began to reflect the widening of the popular music horizon by showing signs of specialisation, notably in its bias towards African music, reggae and American post-punk.

That tendency has become a guiding tenet of the latest collection; his reviews are much less immediate and more complex than in the 70s or 80s, and his scope is accordingly more refined and outré. Christgau is addressing an educated, exclusive New York audience, and one criticism of his most recent work is that he seems to have abandoned the effort to communicate to a mass audience. His prose now requires as much concentration as the music which inspires his most intelligent writing: Christgau would take that as a compliment.

But even if Christgau's preference for Le Tigre and Tom Ze over Oasis and Marilyn Manson doesn't chime with your own tastes, his book is valuable merely for its introduction – in which he not only explains his methods, but ponders the value of the critic in an age when it is impossible for any single listener to keep track of the babble of popular music.

"I probably take active pleasure in more records than any critic out there", he boasts, a New Yorker to the manner born. But his arrogance doesn't prevent him from listening – expanding his knowledge by venturing into previously unvisited pockets of world music or pop, and daring to be surprised by a rare moment of passion from a Paul McCartney or a Garth Brooks.

Most of all, his book is a spirited riposte to those professional nostalgists (and I've been one of them, often enough) who carp that the music doesn't matter the way it used to, that it has lost its sense of mainstream political engagement and cultural signposting. In place of those vanishing values, Christgau offers the compensation of "a democratic cornucopia", a hubbub of voices and styles that defy categorisation or ghettoisation. If Larkin's book would be an ideal reference source for an inquisitive teenager, and *The Mojo Collection* for a literate graduate, then *Christgau's Record Guide* might be the preferred travelling companion for a jaded soul eager to rediscover the intellectual and emotional pleasures once readily available from mainstream popular music, but which now have to be retrieved from the furthest reaches of our global culture.

A NEW AGE OF CRITICISM

And where does that leave Paul Williams? The founder of *Crawdaddy* magazine in the 60s, the writer of maybe two dozen books, notably 1968's *Outlaw Blues* and two (soon three) volumes of *Bob Dylan: Performing Artist*, Williams has pioneered a transformation in the role of the rock critic – from musical chaperon to new age guru.

The 20th Century's Greatest Hits: A Top 40 List (Forge, £13.95) is either, depending on your taste, the ultimate descent of cultural criticism into sentimental banality; or an inspirational guide to the spiritual potential of great art; or, quite possibly, both.

And what exactly is great art? Williams claims that it "is not some objective phenomenon; it is an essentially subjective, and often profoundly spiritual, personal experience". Great art, then, is art that appears great to the viewer – a thesis so simple, or simplistic, that it threatens to make both opinionated (Christgau) and outwardly objective (*Mojo*) critics redundant. As his volumes on Dylan illustrate, Williams can only respond to art in the most personal sense: he cherishes the idea

that even the most famous artworks of the last century might become "your secret treasure". Beyond even that, he declares that "Art exists not so much in the moment when it is created as in the moment when it is received". If a tree falls in the forest but no one hears, does the tree really fall? If Bob Dylan releases an album but no one buys it, does the album really exist? Of such Zen paradoxes are Williams' current career made.

So any objection to his selection of artistic icons on the grounds of taste and judgement is immediately rendered irrelevant. In a sense, *The 20th Century's Greatest Hits* is not, as the cover blurb suggests, an exploration of "What works of art should be remembered, and why?", but a sly form of autobiography. It tells the story of an inquisitive teenager in the late 50s, obsessed with the infinite mental space of sci-fi and the universal beneficence of the Declaration of Human Rights, who falls under the spell of beat poetry and hence Bob Dylan, is psychedelized into the land of the Grateful Dead, and emerges to contemplate the quiet mysteries of Buddhism and the I-Ching (not to forget that Zen master, Winnie The Pooh). The fact that he also loves Patti Smith and the Velvet Underground can be attributed to the fact that even the most generous spirit needs sometimes to engage with the squalor of the physical world.

In this mental landscape, it matters not a jot that Williams has never read James Joyce's *Ulysses*. (He is the critic, after all, who began his study of Neil Young by admitting that he had never heard several of Young's records.) "Great writers need great readers," he declares. "I can praise the reader of *Ulysses* unashamedly, because I'm not talking about myself."

Williams occupies a world where everything is sunshine, every event is serendipity, every encounter with art is potentially life-enhancing. He is a critic who never criticises, but who searches endlessly for the positive. Idealistic, impassioned and almost idiotically optimistic, his writing is chicken soup for the weary soul, no matter how appalled one's intellect might be by his mushy-headed sentimentality. His ideal reader would be 17 years old, and prepared to fall headlong in love with Williams' utopian vision of human potential.

So it's easy to imagine Williams – and indeed Larkin and Christgau – in the guise of teacher. If Larkin is the easy-going but slightly baffled spectator of high-spirited adolescents, then Williams is the general studies lecturer who inspires his students to protest against the trashing of a local beauty spot (and is immortalised in a Disney TV movie). Christgau is the terrifying highbrow, rapier-fast with his wit and destroying the illusions of all but a few favourite pupils, who can't quite understand what they've done to deserve his attention. And *The Mojo Collection*? That's the school library, under enlightened stewardship.

Or, of course, you can skip school entirely, and find your own way through the world. You might even be inspired to write a book about it.

A SINGULAR SONG:
BERT JANSCH AND THE FOLK TAPESTRY

Weighty subtitles can be a painless way for a writer to lend their work some gravitas, but with *Dazzling Stranger: Bert Jansch And The British Folk And Blues Revival* (Bloomsbury, £25), Colin Harper more than justifies any expectations. In essence, this compelling and superbly researched narrative is two books in one: a vivid and expansive portrait of the fiercely combative British folk scene from the early 50s to the mid-60s, and then a poignant biography of the man whom Harper views as the most significant survivor of that chaos. As **Peter Doggett** discovered, the saga of the book's genesis was almost as protracted as the story it tells.

dazzling stranger
bert jansch and the
british folk and blues
revival colin harper

How did your original plan for a Pentangle book in the early 90s mutate into a Bert Jansch biography, almost a decade later?

It's a long story! Bert has been a hero of mine ever since I saw a film of a Pentangle performance from Belgium in 1972, which was most curiously re-broadcast on Ulster TV in the early 80s. I was still at school, and I was really attracted to this music from a deeply distant era. I gradually began trawling round secondhand shops in search of Pentangle and Jansch albums, at a time when there were no reissues around, and the originals were really difficult to find – let alone any information about these people.

During 1990-91 I had some down-time after finishing a degree in History, and decided I wanted to write a book about Pentangle. It seemed like it would be a finite thing to do, a compact story. So I spent a lot of time interviewing various people in the group and outside – among them Bert Jansch, who I found to be most enigmatic.

But I soon discovered that one of the group, Danny Thompson, was very much against the project. He – justifiably, in many ways – feels that he was ripped off during the Pentangle era, and consequently associated my activities with that negativity. I understand he refers to the band as 'the P-word' these days. The idea of continuing with the book under those circumstances upset me. So, barring some fairly lengthy sleevenotes for the first wave of Jansch and Pentangle CD reissues, I put all the work that I had done aside.

Several years later, as I explain in the book, I was actually driving Bert across Ireland after a gig – we had got to know each other reasonably well over the years – when suddenly, completely out of the blue, he asked if I would consider reviving the book idea. Previously, he hadn't taken any particular interest in my project, but I think his current wife Loren had suggested that it would be a good idea. There were a few external circumstances at that particular time which meant it would be possible for me to effectively take a year out of my other work and devote late 1998 and most of 1999 to researching and telling his story – because, to be brutally frank about it, the kind of advances available for this kind of book simply don't cover the period of time required.

Did you actually have a contract with a publisher for the Pentangle book?
No, I had approached several publishers in the early 90s, but I got very negative responses. So I was very pleasantly surprised in 1998, when I resurrected the idea as a book about Bert Jansch, that the response was much more positive. Bert

had enjoyed both a commercial and creative renaissance during the intervening period, and there had been books on other, equally left-field, or marginal, or however you want to describe it, figures like Alexis Korner and Nick Drake. In a way, publishing had caught up with the CD revolution, which had led thousands of people to go back to the music of the past and regard these guys as legends, not old has-beens. Also, my own CV – and hopefully also my actual ability – as a writer had a good deal more credibility by this point.

Between 1991 and 1998, were you still researching Pentangle material?
I became a professional writer during that period, in 1994 – feature-writing and reviewing for various national newspapers and magazines. I'd also acquired a post-grad in Information Management, as a somewhat extreme reaction to meeting Kim Fowley and feeling a need to balance my fraternisings with 60s weirdos with something unashamedly pedestrian! As it happens, I'm currently pursuing a few opportunities in various archives and libraries, so it might all have a happy ending.

Anyway, through my journalistic activities I'd been lucky enough to meet lots of people who were part of the Jansch story, like Ralph McTell, Roy Harper, Anne Briggs, Wizz Jones; so I was inadvertently building up a library of relevant interview material.

When you were approaching people for interviews explicitly for the book, was there any sense of bitterness from Bert's contemporaries that you were writing about him rather than them?
There was no jealousy at all – something which I think last year's tribute album,

People On The Highway (Market Square Records), bears out. Bert is held in total awe by people: even by people he's been married to! Even John Renbourn, who obviously had some kind of falling-out with Bert during a US tour together in the early 90s, is still effusive about Bert's talent. It wasn't just his stature as a musician that people respected, but also the fact that there is absolutely no malice about the man. I've scarcely ever heard him say a bad word about anybody.

Yet he has a reputation in the industry for being difficult, or at the very least taciturn, which might make him hard to deal with.
It's certainly very hard to get close to him in a conventional way. He's very generous, very good-hearted, but he's also a solitary and singular man. That doesn't make him rude, merely distanced in a way that other people sometimes find unsettling. I think people expect too much from artists who are blessed, or cursed, with exceptional creative desire, and who, like Bert, can't turn it off. But I also feel that his recent marriage to Loren has allowed other people to have more normal relationships with him.

You found a wonderful quote from an old interview with Bert: "I've got a very bad memory for things I don't want to remember". That doesn't make him sound like the ideal interviewee.
Well, Bert isn't really interested in his own past. He's a genuine enigma, there is no other way of putting it. For instance, he doesn't even have copies of his own records. I think that reading the draft of the book – out of courtesy, I gave him the chance to say if there was anything he

really objected to in the manuscript, and all he removed were literally two factual inaccuracies – was very cathartic for him. He's never been particularly aware of his reviews, or what people had to say about him, so that was probably quite revealing for him.

We sat down for two very substantial series of interview sessions during the year of writing, and Bert did his best to remember stuff. But it was at least as important, if not more so, for me to collect together all the previously published interviews with him, particularly those from the distant past, as they certainly filled various yawning chasms in his memory!

The first half of the book deals with the British folk scene in the 50s and early 60s as a landscape; the second half is a tight close-up on Jansch's career since then. Why the shift in perspective?
When I began writing the book, I had two role models in mind: Harry Shapiro's biography of Alexis Korner, another cult figure, which I thought was very tightly written; and Humphrey Carpenter's *The Inklings*, which inspired me as an example of how to weave together a narrative out of several interlinked but separate stories.

I was aware as I was researching the book that the pre-history of the folk scene had never been chronicled before, and that there were loads of characters who had peripheral, or sometimes major, roles in Bert's story, who deserved to be documented in more detail – but who would probably never get a book of their own. So the landscape approach was a way of giving them their proper place in history.

You'll notice that the point where I narrow the focus was at the start of Pentangle. In fact, I virtually skate over the most successful middle years of their career, for the reason I've already mentioned, that one of the band really didn't want their story to be told. So I concentrated entirely on Bert's activities during that time, and that set me up for the second half of the book, from Bert's early 70s solo 'comeback' onwards, when anyway the folk scene was more diffuse than it had been the previous decade.

Perhaps the key issue is whether Bert Jansch is actually the most central figure in that folk scene, as well as in your biography.
That's a good question! He certainly is in the sense that he seems to cover all the different areas I was writing about. His career began in the 50s, and it takes in London and Edinburgh, the two cities I focus on. Bert was also one of the first singers to go travelling round Europe. Then he was certainly regarded as the key figure in London between 1965-1967; he was like a hipper version of Donovan.

In another way, Bert is the key representative of the British singer-songwriter tradition: in fact, he's probably the first of the line. Obviously, when you look at the traditional end of the folk scene, then Martin Carthy was a more important figure among revival singers; he was the one who brought that music into a modern context. But in terms of contemporary music, Bert was the man.

You mentioned that you let Bert Jansch see the manuscript before publication. Were you concerned that might prejudice your independence as a writer?
Not at all, because he had already given me carte blanche to speak to whoever I wanted, and just get on with it. In fact, Bert

wasn't the only person who read the book. I sent out copies of the relevant chapters to several of the main participants, and also to important observers like the journalist and author Karl Dallas, and almost let them 'referee' some of the disputes. I think that added to the accuracy and detail of the book in the end, rather than detracting from it. It certainly didn't add up to any kind of censorship of what I was writing.

Incidentally, I dedicated the book to Karl Dallas – who championed folk music of all shades for *Melody Maker* and the various specialist journals he founded and edited during the 60s and 70s – because I felt quite strongly that people like me, and indeed yourself, are only able to write these kind of books because people like him went the extra mile in the detail and veracity of their reporting and interviewing at the time. Had he been in it purely for the money, Karl could have got away with an awful lot less as a writer – and history would have been very much poorer as a result.

Given that Jansch is, in publishing terms at least, a marginal figure, did you have any problems getting such a substantial book past your publisher?
Overall, I had a very constructive relationship with them, and I'm very pleased with the finished book. But I did have to make some sacrifices along the way.

My original deal was for 110,000 words, with a verbal agreement with the editor who signed the deal that I could go to 140,000 words. Unfortunately he left Bloomsbury, a new editor was appointed – and I submitted a manuscript that was 200,000 words long! Even getting it down to that point meant cutting out a series of massive appendices, including discographical material, lists of Bert's radio sessions, and so on.

I think in retrospect that Bloomsbury wanted another book like Patrick Humphries' biography of Nick Drake, which would be a nice linear narrative about one man. But I was determined that the book would also be the story of the Folk Revival. Under the circumstances, I think we came to a very good accommodation. They appointed an excellent text editor, and between us we trimmed the book back from 200,000 words to 175,000 – which I'm happy to concede was an improvement. There was a slightly tense moment after that when Bloomsbury were suggesting further cuts, but I put my foot down and said, no, this is the book.

Cover price had been the imperative, but even with all the editing it still had to go out at £25, which understandably concerned some at Bloomsbury; but, to their credit, they accepted the 175,000-word version and went with it. I'm sure the price

tag has affected sales to *some* extent but, sales wise, I'm delighted to say it's comfortably outstripping their targets.

And this has obviously given you the taste for biographies...
Well, yes and no! I did promise my wife 'never again', but somehow I've found myself collaborating with Andy Irvine at the moment on a book which I'm describing as "a biographically-assisted memoir". So it's not quite the Irish equivalent of the Bert book, but it will cover the 60s folk scene in Ireland, centred around Andy's immediate circle, Sweeney's Men, and so on.

I'm also helping Duffy Power make his first record for 25 years, which is a direct spin-off of the book and tribute album. I think he's one of the great lost talents of British music, so I was very pleased to be able to write about his work in the Bert book – and thrilled to be helping him make music again. It's very exciting. Who knows, we might even make some money!

ALL TOGETHER NOW?
THE BEATLES ANTHOLOGY

by John Robertson

THE BEATLES recorded everything from 'Love Me Do' to *Abbey Road* in seven years. Three decades later, it's taken them longer than that to finish a book. *Anthology* must surely be the most-delayed TV tie-in in publishing history. Many of its interviews were taped in 1992; the TV series reached our screens in late 1995; but the accompanying book didn't surface until November 2000.

One crucial reason for the postponement was the death of Derek Taylor in the summer of 1997. Taylor, the Beatles' urbane, calm and almost impossibly charming PR representative, was the only man on the planet who could have persuaded all three surviving Beatles to agree on a text that would sum up their increasingly contentious mutual history. Although he died long before the project was completed, every page of the *Anthology* bears the stamp of his peerless prose.

Given the task of mollifying four giant egos (with Yoko Ono acting as the guardian of her late husband's interests) and an even more enormous corporate entity, the creators of the *Anthology* faced an almost impossible task. Many critics (myself included) expected that this much-vaunted book would be a banal, bland whitewash over the Beatles' tempestuous career,

smoothing out disagreements and accentuating the unity of (in Ringo Starr's immortal, tear-stained phrase) "four guys who loved each other so much".

Remarkably, the *Anthology* succeeds in presenting the Beatles both as an idealistic force of nature, and as an uneasy truce between four over-stimulated imaginations. Though its message is peace and love, snapshots of open warfare flash from many of its pages, interrupted by cynical bursts of sarcasm (particularly from the ever droll and endlessly quotable George Harrison).

No book of this nature could ever satisfy all tastes: among the obvious omissions are (for the prurient) the group's sexual adventures on tour and the vicious legal battle in the High Court after their split; and (for the pedantic) any mention of their 1968 hit single, 'Lady Madonna'.

But to balance every churlish complaint, there should be a chorus of praise for the way in which Derek Taylor and the Genesis Publications editorial team sequenced and embroidered such a vast tapestry of material – more than 300,000 words, mostly drawn from specially conducted interviews with McCartney, Harrison and Starr, and augmented by the pick of a lifetime's loquaciousness from the lips of John Lennon. Scholars will be decoding this manuscript for years; here we single out some of the richest pickings.

I'M A LOSER

*The Mysterious Disappearance
of Pete Best*

In August 1962, drummer Pete Best was ousted from the Beatles, days before they were due to record their debut single. His sacking triggered a mini-rebellion from their fans – one of whom duly blacked George Harrison's eye at the Cavern Club – and set in motion a rumour industry that has flourished ever since. The scandal has already prompted two disappointingly vague autobiographies by Best himself (*Beatle!* and *The Best Years Of The Beatles*), plus an entertaining and provocative piece of investigative journalism by Spencer Leigh (*Drummed Out*).

But the Beatles themselves have chosen to be altogether more reticent about this distasteful episode. Ever since Best launched a libel suit against his replacement, Ringo Starr, over comments made in a 1965 *Playboy* interview (where Starr alleged falsely that Best had been expelled from the group because of problems with drugs), the group have maintained a stony profile whenever the topic has been raised. In the *Anthology* TV series, for instance, Best's departure was glossed as a minor hiccup, an inevitable substitution to allow Starr into their ranks. In his official biography, *Many Years From Now*, McCartney allowed Miles simply to suggest that "it was a question of attitude. Pete was moody and did not fit in that well with the other three."

As usual whenever there is devious manouevring afoot, Paul McCartney has been targetted as the most likely instigator of Best's elimination. The motive, appar-

ently, was jealousy: as McCartney admits in *Anthology*, "(Pete) was a good-looking guy, and out of all the people in the group, the girls used to go for him". But John Lennon had little time for this suggestion: "The myth built up over the years that he was great and Paul was jealous of him because he was pretty." Instead, Lennon contended that Best "was a harmless guy, but he was not quick. All of us had quick minds, but he never picked that up."

Elsewhere, McCartney states both that "He was a good drummer" and "We knew that he wasn't that good a player"; and he recalls that "I used to get on Pete's case a bit" in Hamburg: "He'd often stay out all night. He got to know a stripper … She didn't finish work until four, so he'd stay up with her and roll back at about ten in the morning, and be going to bed when we were starting work. I think that had something to do with a rift starting."

Like an itch they can't quite scratch, the Beatles return again and again to this incident in *Anthology*. "Pete would never hang out with us," George Harrison insists. McCartney picks up the point: "It was a personality thing … He was slightly different to the rest of us, not quite as studenty." The fact that Ringo Starr scarcely attended school because of illness, and struck most onlookers, the Beatles included, as a totally unstudenty and forbidding Teddy Boy, seems to have eluded him.

Changing tack, McCartney lights on the group's June 1962 audition with Parlophone, when producer George Martin expressed his unhappiness with Best's playing: "George took us to one side and said, 'I'm really unhappy with the drummer. Would you consider changing him?' We said, 'No, we can't!'" It was one of those terrible things you go through as kids. Can we betray him? No. But our career was on the line … It was strictly a professional decision."

But it is Harrison – in Lennon's absence, now easily the most outspoken member of the Beatles – who finally settles the question, and proudly takes credit for the dirty deed: "To me it was apparent. Pete kept being sick and not showing up for gigs, so we would get Ringo to sit in with the band instead, and every time Ringo sat in, it seemed like 'this is it'. I was quite responsible for stirring things up. I conspired to get Ringo in for good. I talked to Paul and John until they came round to the idea." So nearly 40 years after he was removed from the Beatles, Pete Best finally knows who to blame.

I'M SO TIRED
The boring of the Beatles

Keith Badman's intensely detailed and valuable *The Beatles: Off The Record* (Omnibus, £19.95), cannily published weeks before the *Anthology*, is an oral chronology of the group's history, based entirely on contemporary newspaper cuttings and radio interviews, without the distortions of hindsight. What's shocking, in retrospect, as you trawl through hundreds of pages of press conference transcripts and lively quips to local *Gazettes* and *Daily Posts* across Britain, is how early disillusionment with the entire Beatles project surfaces in the words of George Harrison – who by 1966 had his sights firmly set on the Himalayas, and his ears tuned to the hypnotic drone of the sitar.

Even more surprising is the fact that the *Anthology* reflects that encroaching ennui so faithfully. Looking back at their first full US tour in 1964, Harrison recalls that

"With the concerts and Beatlemania, after a while the novelty wore off and then it was very boring. It wasn't just the noise on stage, not hearing the music and playing the same old songs, it was too much everywhere we went."

Jaded at just 23, Harrison is quoted in *Anthology* speaking in 1966, the year of *Revolver* and *Pet Sounds*, *Blonde On Blonde* and *Aftermath*, the birth of Hendrix and the Velvet Underground, the dawn of psychedelia, the creative peak of Motown and Atlantic soul, and the year most often selected as the most important in rock history: "To me, (Indian music) is the only really great music now, and it makes Western three-or-four-beat type stuff seem somehow dead."

John Lennon was equally weary in 1966 of life as a Beatle: "We are all old men … What I have done is fine, but now I have to do something else. We sort of half hope for The Downfall, a nice downfall. Then we would just be a pleasant memory." And another quote from that year sheds a sombre light on his attitude to the Beatles: "There's something else I'm going to do, something I must do – only I don't know what it is. That's why I go round painting and taping and drawing and writing and that, because it may be one of them. All I know is, this isn't it for me."

THE INNER LIGHT
Acid cuts through the Fab Four

If George Harrison ever needs a career, he should consider the life of a salesman. Here he is on the acid experience: "You suddenly experience the soul as free and unbound … You're not feeling intoxicated, you're straight, with a twist – taken out of focus. Suddenly you can see walls and you can see your body as if it isn't a solid … It's amazing … It must be like that for people who have attained a 'cosmic consciousness' … LSD gave me the experience of 'I am not this body. I am pure energy soaring about everywhere."

This gushing enthusiasm is a recent quote, dating from more than 30 years after he visited the supposed centre of San Francisco acid culture, and realised: "It wasn't what I thought – spiritual awakenings and being artistic – it was like alcoholism, like any addiction … That was the turning-point for me – that's when I went off the whole drug cult."

Though John Lennon's repeated bouts of heroin use in the late 60s are discreetly omitted from the *Anthology*, the group's whole-hearted endorsement of lysergic acid is reflected in glorious detail. In a culture where timidity usually conquers truthfulness on the subject of illegal drugs, the Beatles' outspoken honesty is refreshing.

Equally blatant is the tension that Harrison and Lennon's chemical enlightenment caused within the previously tight-knit group. "John and I had decided that Paul and Ringo had to have acid," Harrison remarks of their 1965 US tour, "because we couldn't relate to them any more. Not just on the one level – we couldn't relate to them on *any* level, because acid had changed us so much." Ringo Starr happily went along for the trip – "I'd take anything", he says today – but Paul McCartney was more reticent. "Paul felt very out of it," Lennon is quoted as saying, "because we are all slightly cruel: 'We're taking it and you're not'."

Harrison highlights their shared acid experience as the birthplace of a new relationship between himself and Lennon: "John and I spent a lot of time together from then on, and I felt closer to him than

all the others, right through until his death … just by the look in his eyes I felt we were connected." (There is no hint, incidentally, that Lennon reciprocated this feeling; in his 1980 *Playboy* interview, he voiced little but contempt for Harrison.)

While McCartney remained isolated from the other Beatles in London, exploring avant-garde theatre and *musique concrete*, Harrison, Lennon and Starr retired to their stockbroker belt mansions in 1965 and 1966, to contemplate the chemically-induced infinite. Even then, their responses varied: while Starr saw himself "swimming in jelly in the pool … it was a fabulous day", and Harrison uncovered the origins of the universe, Lennon was gripped by nightmares. Typically, this failed to deter him from continuing his experimentation.

In 1967, McCartney finally joined the acid club, just as Harrison cancelled his membership. Almost immediately, he owned up to his experience on TV. "He always mentioned things like that," Starr notes sardonically. "Once Paul said it, the other three had to deal with it … I could have done without it, myself." Harrison, who was busted for drug possession on McCartney's wedding day in 1969, concurs: "I thought Paul should have been quiet about it. I wish he hadn't said anything, because it made everything messy." And so McCartney's attempt to diminish the growing gulf between himself and the rest of the group merely accentuated the divide.

I ME MINE
Rewriting the writing of history
As even the least studious Beatles follower knows, Lennon and McCartney elected even before they had made a record to

credit all their compositions jointly – with the result, as McCartney is still complaining, that John Lennon's name still appears first in the credits for the most recorded song in history, 'Yesterday', despite the fact he wrote not a single word of it.

While Hunter Davies's 1968 authorised biography (*The Beatles*) continued to pretend that almost all their songs were jointly composed, subsequent interviews allowed Lennon and McCartney to joust over their respective contributions. In 1980, Lennon raised the stakes in *Playboy* by claiming a substantial portion of some of McCartney's finest songs, notably 'Eleanor Rigby' and 'Michelle'; McCartney responded in *Many Years From Now* by seizing key portions of Lennon's 'In My Life'.

With Lennon conveniently unable to call his bluff in *Anthology*, McCartney continues his blitzkrieg strike into his partner's territory. Lennon is quoted as admitting that "Paul helped with the middle eight, musically" of 'In My Life'; McCartney trumps him by reflecting: "Funnily enough, this is one of the only songs John and I disagree on. I remember writing the melody on a mellotron that was parked on his half-landing." He recaptures 'Eleanor Rigby' with a confident "I wrote ... I'd written ...", allowing Lennon only a lame reprisal: "'Eleanor Rigby' was Paul's baby, and I helped with the education of the child."

Not even pausing for breath, McCartney moves on towards his enemy's citadel. Lennon died assuming that he'd written 100 percent of the group's 1966 B-side, 'Rain'. In *Many Years From Now*, McCartney tilted the balance to "70-30 to John"; now he declares baldly that "We sat down and wrote it together ... what gave it its character was collaboration."

Surely there could be no such dispute over 'Lucy In The Sky With Diamonds', inspired by a painting by Lennon's son Julian, and recalled by Lennon and Starr alike as a Lennon creation? Not according to McCartney: "We ... wrote the song, swapping psychedelic suggestions as we went. I remember coming up with 'cellophane' flowers and 'newspaper taxis', and John answered with things like 'kaleidoscope eyes' and 'looking glass ties'." Another decade, and he'll probably be claiming 'The Ballad Of John And Yoko' and 'Imagine' as well.

In 1980, Lennon also suggested that Harrison only managed to write songs like 'Taxman' with his assistance. Two decades on, Harrison can retaliate, claiming that he made equally vital (and equally uncredited) contributions to Lennon songs like 'She Said, She Said'.

Had Lennon lived, the stage would have been set for the three middle-aged men to squabble over their legacy. Human nature? Undoubtedly. Petty-minded? Certainly. But it's also a reminder that the process of creating the Beatles' records was more collaborative than any of the group is perhaps prepared to admit.

HELP!

One man's junta is another man's paradise

In 1967, the Beatles journeyed to Greece (then newly under the control of a fascist military junta) to buy themselves an island – one of many fanciful schemes for the four men and their immediate families to hide themselves away from the rest of the world and live in perfect harmony (at least until it was time to share out the writing royalties). Fortunately for them, and the Greek generals, the plan was abandoned when the acid trip wore off. Always the least starry-eyed of the quartet, Ringo Starr comments: "That was what happened when we got out. It was safer making records, because once they let us out we'd go barmy."

I DON'T WANT TO SPOIL THE PARTY
The slow death of the Beatles

One minute they wanted to spend the rest of their lives together on a Greek island; the next, they couldn't stand to be in the same room. The slide from collective euphoria to mutual dislike occupied less than two years of the Beatles' lives. *Anthology* pricks every raw nerve exposed along the way, without suggesting a more sinister motive for their disagreements than the natural divergence of teenage pals who are maturing at different speeds.

The death of manager Brian Epstein in August 1967 has often been cited as the spark of the group's decline. Looking back, Ringo Starr recalls that "We were still as close to Brian as we had been in the early days"; but his colleagues take a bleaker view. George Harrison contends that "Brian hadn't really done anything since we stopped touring. He was at a bit of a loss." Paul McCartney agrees that "Brian had become a bit redundant", and admits that he told their one-time mentor, "Look, we don't want to put you out of a job, but we do like doing it ourselves". Obviously nobody told Starr, who imagines an alternative scenario: "If Brian was around today, he would be managing us. If we'd been with Brian, we wouldn't have had to go through Allen Klein to be our own men."

Instead, in Epstein's absence, Apple provided the Beatles with an acidic baptism into adulthood. "The theory", McCartney explains, "had been that we'd put all our affairs into one bundle in our own company. It would be all the things we'd ever wanted to do." Or at least two of them wanted: "It was a bad idea, whoever thought of it", Harrison complains. "It was a lesson to anybody not to have a partnership." Having trashed the hippie philosophy in a single sentence, he continues: "Basically, I think John and Paul got carried away with the idea and blew millions, and Ringo and I just had to go along with it."

Equally contentious, and every bit as much of a *fait accompli*, was the introduction into the Beatles' magic circle of an exotic creature – a woman, no less – called Yoko Ono. Aware that Ono now controls Lennon's quarter of the *Anthology* project, and might veto any violent portrayal of her role, McCartney contents himself with a mild complaint about the way in which Lennon sacrificed the group for his new partner: "John had to have Yoko there. I can't blame him, they were intensely in love, but it was fairly off-putting having her sitting on one of the amps. You wanted to say, 'Excuse me, love – can I turn the volume up?' We were always wondering how to say, 'Could you get off my amp?', without interfering with their relationship." Here's another clue for you, Paul: don't call Yoko Ono "love".

As tempers frayed during the summer-long sessions for 'The White Album' (at which Ono was a frequent distraction), Ringo Starr became the first Beatle to quit the group. "I knew we were in a messed-up stage," he says in *Anthology*. "I couldn't take it anymore. There was no magic and the relationships were terrible … I felt like an outsider. But then I realised that we were *all* feeling like outsiders." Starr quickly returned to the fold, but six months later, Harrison made a break for freedom during the *Let It Be* sessions. Intriguingly, all three surviving Beatles attribute his decision to a quarrel between himself and McCartney (as seen in the *Let It Be* movie), contradicting the evidence of the surviving session tapes, which suggest that it was Lennon and Harrison who were at loggerheads on the day in question.

It was not until September 1969 that John Lennon engineered the decisive split in the band, though new manager Allen Klein persuaded him to keep it quiet. As usual, recollections of this momentous event differ wildly. McCartney remembers that "We paled visibly and our jaws slackened a bit …I didn't know what to say". Starr claims to have been less shocked: "(John) said, 'Well, that's it, lads, let's end it.' And we all said 'yes' …because it *was* ending." Presumably removed to a higher spiritual plane that afternoon, Harrison notes that "I don't remember John saying he wanted to break up the Beatles", but admits that "*Everybody* had tried to leave, so it was nothing new."

In spring 1970, while the Beatles pretended in public that nothing had happened, three of the group invited American producer Phil Spector to prepare their *Let It Be* album for release. McCartney was horrified, then and now: "I heard the Spector version again recently, and it sounded terrible." Thirty years on, this remains the minority view, against Lennon ("he did a great job"), Starr ("I like what Phil did") and Harrison ("I personally thought it was a good idea").

The same battlelines were drawn in April 1970, when McCartney finally told the public what the Beatles had known for several months: the group was finished. Harrison is still bitter about his announcement, which was timed to coincide with

the release of the *McCartney* album: "Paul has a way of using stuff. I mean, even now, if he is going to do a tour he'll conveniently tell the press that we're all getting back together or something. It's just his way, really." The accusation rankles with McCartney: "The others all saw me as the one who issued the statements, as if it was to my advantage. But all I did on the break-up was, unlike them, to tell the truth." Touché …

AND IN THE END ....
Divorce and the single Beatle
John Lennon instigated the Beatles' split, and welcomed it with open arms. Paul McCartney recalls that when he made the announcement to the rest of the group, he was excited, exactly as he had been when he'd left his first wife for Yoko Ono a year earlier.

McCartney himself took the news much harder. "I really got the feeling of being redundant," he says in *Anthology*. "It was about self-worth. I just suddenly felt I wasn't worth anything if it wasn't in the Beatles … I took to my bed, didn't bother shaving much, did a lot of drinking … I lost the plot there for a little while – about a year, actually."

Ringo Starr's response was more ambiguous. At the same moment that he concedes that "It was a relief when we finally said we would split up," he admits: "I sat in my garden for a while wondering what the hell to do with my life … It was quite a dramatic period for me – or *traumatic*, actually."

George Harrison had for years been the least committed of the Beatles to their continued existence, and he was already looking beyond the merely physical to a more comfortable dimension: "My feeling when we went our separate ways was to enjoy the space that it gave me, the space to be able to think at my own speed." And it is Harrison who supplies the most telling comment about life as a Beatle, the resonance of which echoes back through *Anthology* to the very first page: "(The Beatles) looked like such a great thing to be in. And it *was*. But it was also a great thing to get out of."

ACROSS THE GREAT DIVIDE: COUNTRY AND ROCK

by Debbie Cassell

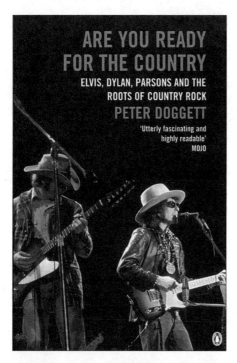

AFTER YEARS of being marginalised by rock historians, country music has inspired a flurry of literary activity in recent months. While Brian Hinton's *Country Roads* (Sanctuary, £12.99) takes a long country ramble through the genre's history (and his own record collection), and John Einarson's *Desperados* (Cooper Square Press) concentrates firmly on the decade-long saga of classic country-rock, Peter Doggett's *Are You Ready For The Country* (Viking, £12.99) is an attempt to trace and understand the long and often turbulent relationship between rock and country.

Eschewing a chronological approach, Doggett's book begins with Bob Dylan joining Johnny Cash on American TV in 1969, a moment which he sees as emblematic of the tension between the two genres. He then returns to the birth of what we now know as country-rock, around 1964, tracking its brief rise and painful decline through to the late 70s.

The second section of his book reverses chronology again, balancing the rock orientation of the opening chapters by focusing on how country music first spawned, and then distanced itself from, rock'n'roll in the 50s, before engaging in a series of increasingly controversial encounters with its illegitimate child.

Are You Ready For The Country ends with a sequence of thematic chapters which document the many discrete battlegrounds on which the two genres have fought over the last 25 years, from Southern redneck rock and New Country to punk and alt country. **Debbie Cassell** quizzed Doggett about the book, and the cultural philosophy behind it.

How did you get ready for the country?
By overcoming my own prejudices. We seem to grow up in Britain – or certainly in England – with an innate prejudice against country music. People complain that it's sentimental, that it's clichéd, and that it's shallow. But what's at the root of their misgivings is the fact that it's the music of the white American South, and that is a culture which – for very good reason – is instantly associated in people's minds with racial bigotry, rural simplicity, the Ku Klux Klan, a whole sheaf of attitudes that range from backward to fascist.

So I had two separate kinds of prejudice to overcome – against the music, and against the culture. I won the first battle by listening to artists that I loved as a teenager, everyone from Jerry Lee Lewis to Bob Dylan, via the Stones and the Byrds, and realising that country was a major part of what they were doing. In the case of someone like Jerry Lee, he's a country boy first and foremost, and he's picked up virtually all the baggage of the South along the way, good and bad.

It's too easy to say that country is the white man's blues, but there's an element of truth in that, and when you get beyond your knee-jerk reaction – that these guys sound like hillbillies, and so they must all be stupid racists – you can start to appreciate that the best country music has soul. Sure, there's plenty of bad country, which is sentimental and sickly. But there's plenty of bad rock out there, as well. I wouldn't go to the stake for ELP or Spandau Ballet or even Oasis, thanks very much.

The more I listened to country, the more I noticed when other people wrote books that were supposed to be wide-ranging histories of popular music – and they'd miss country out. Lucy O'Brien's *She Bop* is a good example. It's a great book, but although she chronicles every possible permutation of women playing black music, she acts like country never existed. So one of the main impulses for *Are You Ready For The Country* was to set the record straight.

I mentioned that I had to overcome my prejudice against Southern culture, and I did that by spending a lot of time there. That doesn't mean I ended up as an apologist for slavery or discrimination, just that I appreciated that they have a distinct culture of their own, which has been shaped by their own battles against prejudice. We associate the white South with racism; but much of the rest of America seems to hold the same prejudices against the South that whites there have traditionally held against blacks.

As an Englishman who has spent nearly all his life living in the Home Counties, what made you think you could analyse roots music from the Deep South?
Arrogance! Not entirely, though there's a strong element of that in everyone who forces their opinions on the public. I felt as an outsider it was easier for me to chart all the shifts of culture and music which made up the story of my book. I wasn't starting from one side of the divide or the other; most importantly, I wasn't trying to make either side the winner.

Ironically, your question is almost exactly the reason why the American branch of Viking/Penguin originally turned down the chance to publish the book there – though they've since relented, and it's coming out later this year. Who the hell *is* this Brit? Well, hopefully he's somebody who has listened to the music with open ears, and listened to what the musicians had to say in the same spirit.

You mentioned earlier the 'soul' of country music: do you think that has actually less to do with the music itself than with nostalgia for some kind of almost puritanical return to basic values?

As Neil Young sang, "Even Richard Nixon has got soul" – and Nixon was a country fan! I wouldn't like to define what soul is, but once you learn how to listen to it, you can find emotional commitment, and integrity, and passion, in any kind of music, and country is no exception. It mightn't be there in every song, any more than it is in black music. But listen to George Jones, Willie Nelson, Hank Williams, Randy Travis – every one of them is a soul singer in my head.

I think your other idea, the nostalgia for rural values, is a very important element in country music, both for its natural audience in the States, and also for visitors from the weird world of rock, who probably reckon that they're being inducted into a twilight world of gothic Americana every time they hear a steel guitar. Most people in the South live in cities, like they do in the rest of the Western world. But most of that migration has happened within living memory, the same way as it did with the black blues singers who left the South in search of work in Chicago or Detroit. So it's a shared memory for everyone in the culture. Sometimes they look back on it with fondness, sometimes they're glad they got out of there in one piece.

When is a country song a country song, and not a blues or a folk song?
Oh God. Musicologists could probably tell you which melodic patterns, and chord changes, and tempos, are definitively 'country'. But I can't tell you that. What I do know is that I can recognise a country song when I hear one. That might be because it's a white man's blues, as the cliché has it, or because it's sung with a Southern twang, or because it has a steel guitar and a fiddle on it, or because it uses the language of ordinary people to talk about ordinary people's problems, or because it has the same chord changes as an old Hank Williams song. Or it might have none of those things.

So maybe I'm saying that country is as much a state of mind as it is a set of musical rules. When Willie Nelson sings 'Georgia On My Mind', you could say that it's country, or blues, or jazz, or easy listening, or even (God help us) lounge music. But Willie thinks it's country, and that's good enough for me.

In your introduction, you ask whether 'country, the music of the white American South, can reach across America, and out into the world, without losing its soul?' and whether rock music can be fed by it without 'becoming trapped in the culture from which it originated'. Can country music retain its essence and transcend its origins?
Well, I could write a book about that. In fact, I think I already did. In a way, I'd almost rather let the individual musicians who are covered in the book answer that question for you.

I think the accurate answer is a mixture of yes and no that varies from case to case. For instance, I make the point that when country flirts with Hollywood – which it does every five years, almost as if it's programmed into the genes – it's in danger of losing its identity in a way which rock musicians would never even consider, or worry about. But it can always find its way back home by remembering that it wasn't born in Hollywood.

How did you decide who the influential figures in your story were? For instance, Buddy Holly is hardly mentioned in the book (refreshingly perhaps), while Michael Nesmith, who is undeniably gifted but far less celebrated, claims two chapters.

Yes, I had a tough job getting that past my editor at Penguin. I had to buy him a Nesmith CD! Most of the influential figures chose themselves, like Dylan or Presley or Gram Parsons or Emmylou Harris, because their influence has been so apparent down the years. But Michael Nesmith is fascinating because he was making intelligent country-rock records before Parsons; and by 1968, he was starting to flirt with avant-garde influences in a way that no one has really picked up on. He wasn't a pioneer, because nobody chose to follow his example, but he was certainly an innovator.

Buddy Holly is a major figure in rock history, but he had a very minimal influence on country until the 80s and 90s. He started out playing straight hillbilly music, but he had knocked almost all of those influences out of his sound by the time he started making hit records. That's why he doesn't get as much coverage in the book as Elvis or Jerry Lee.

Why do you think country music became so difficult to sell as soon as Elvis Presley and Bill Haley came along in the mid-50s?

Because a lot of popular music back then, even country music, was basically teen music – and the teens wanted somebody with a backbeat and a pumping pelvis.

Don't forget that most of those rockers spent their first couple of years on the road playing with country artists, not pop. You might as well ask why it was so tough for American balladeers to sell records once the Beatles turned up. The times had changed, and the old guys suddenly sounded old.

Why do you cite Dylan's appearance on the Johnny Cash Show as the pivotal flashpoint of rock and country?

In musical terms, I actually don't think it is that pivotal. Its impact came from the fact that you had the hottest country star in America, and the most compelling rock icon of the 60s, sharing a stage and singing country tunes together. And it was on national TV in the States – though not here, because the BBC didn't think their performance was good enough!

Other people had been making country-rock records by then for at least three years, but Dylan was the one who took it into the pop mainstream. That's why I wanted to start the book that way – plus the fact that it's such a great story, which starts with Bob trudging through a blizzard to knock on Roy Orbison's door.

Weren't the Everly Brothers the first country rock band?

No, that was Elvis, Scotty & Bill. Or maybe Bill Haley and his Saddlemen. But if you listen to the country albums the Everlys made in the early 60s, they sure sound a lot like Gram Parsons and the International Submarine Band.

Gram Parsons' music has been overshadowed by his legend in the last few years, but you redress the balance here. How important a figure was

Parsons, in your opinion, in the rise and fall of country rock?

If he'd lived, I don't think he would be anything more than a minor cult figure – albeit one who helped to create one of the greatest rock albums of the 60s, the Burritos' *Gilded Palace Of Sin*. And of course we don't know what he would have done with another 10 or 20 years at his disposal.

But I think his main influence has been as an icon, for subsequent generations – and then only among rock musicians. I asked Waylon Jennings about him, and he said he couldn't see what all the fuss was about, and that there were plenty better country singers than Gram. And he's right. What Gram added was rock decadence, rock sensibility, rock arrogance and a classic rock death. That's not to say I don't love his music, because I do, but I also think he's more renowned for being Gram Parsons than he is for singing like Gram Parsons. To put it another way, he's not as adventurous a country-rock musician as another ex-member of the Byrds, Gene Clark, but Gene doesn't have that aura about him.

Tragically, nearly everyone over the age of 30 has, at one time or another, either owned or spilt beer over an Eagles album. Such nice boys, and yet you don't seem to like them very much – what's your problem? Surely the Eagles epitomise country rock?

They epitomise what people came to *think* was country rock, which is slick 70s Los Angeles rock with CSNY harmonies. Aside from their second album, *Desperado*, which I love, there's precious little actual country in their work,

especially after about 1975 when Bernie Leadon left the band. Now, Don Henley has written some magnificent songs, but the Eagles somehow seem to me to encapsulate a corporate arrogance that makes them insufferable. No matter how much I enjoy a lot of their music, I find it hard to distance myself from their image. It's my fault, probably, not theirs. They probably wouldn't like me either.

You convincingly argue that the uneasy relationship between country and rock mirrors the North/South cultural divide. Why do you think that so many rock musicians from the Northern states – Canada, even, in the case of luminaries like Neil Young and Robbie Robertson – have found country so seductive a holy grail, when so many other famous rock figures have disowned it?

Two reasons: maybe they have more open ears than their contemporaries; and secondly because they were entranced by the same combination of 50s country-tinged rock'n'roll and 60s country-rock that pulled me into the music. Someone like Robbie Robertson up in Canada couldn't wait to get down to the South. He wasn't thinking about rednecks, he wanted to go and see Sun Records!

The final section of your book examines the fall-out from the so-called collision of country and rock over the last 25 years. But do you think there is still such a thing as country music beyond the realms of parody and music history?

I think that there will always be country music, even when rock is dead – if it isn't already in the purist sense.

I have a very simplistic, and no doubt deeply flawed, theory to explain this, but

I've found it useful. Rock music clings to the philosophy of permanent revolution. It's always striking out for new ground, trashing the immediate past, trying to be louder and more outrageous and more relevant than its predecessors. Or at least it thinks it is, even while it's playing safe and licking the corporate hand that feeds it.

Country, on the other hand, seems to follow a more circular pattern of history. I think I use the image in the book of a snake with its tail in its mouth. It repeats the same follies every few years, sacrificing all the Southernness that gives it its power and chasing the bright lights of Hollywood. Then it realises what it's done, and comes back home to its roots. That homecoming happened in the mid-60s, when Buck Owens and Merle Haggard came along; in the 70s with the outlaws, like Willie Nelson and Waylon Jennings; in the 80s with Ricky Skaggs and Emmylou Harris; even in the 90s with people like Alan Jackson and Clint Black. It's due to happen again soon. If it hasn't in a couple of years, come back, and I'll try to dream up a better theory!

STONED
THE REBIRTH OF ANDREW OLDHAM
by Johnny Rogan

ALTHOUGH NOT heralded as such on the cover, *Stoned* (Secker & Warburg) is in fact only the first volume of Andrew Oldham's autobiography. The word 'autobiography' may be a misnomer, as the author has utilised a number of different voices to tell his story. As he frankly admits, "There are three sides to every story: yours, mine and the truth". The use of guest voices to provide multiple point of view has been evident in many books in recent years. It's a tricky tactic which can easily fall apart without a strong omniscient narrator. At its worst a book like this can read like a discarded radio or television transcript – a cackle of voices signifying nothing. Faber & Faber's recent *The Brian Epstein Story* underlined some of the flaws, reading less like a book than a collection of quotes from an *Arena* documentary. The cast list was impressive but filmed interviewees seldom prove as enlightening as those taped in private one-to-one conversation.

Even the better autobiographies written in this vein are severely flawed and subject to repetition, verbosity and inadequate editing. Johnny Rotten's *No Irish, No Blacks, No Dogs* contained some cracking anecdotes and priceless revelations, but you still had to wade through rambling repetitious rants and suffer tall tales, petty prejudices and questionable observations. Rotten's typically perverse decision to employ a couple of American ghost writers seemingly unwilling to challenge his melodramatic reminiscences or reading of social history compounded the problem. Among these rock oral histories, David Crosby's unflinching *Long Time Gone*, while fatally lacking a decent appreciation of his music, read superbly, no doubt thanks to his recruitment of scriptwriter friend Carl Gottlieb. Even there, some extremely important voices were conspicuously absent from the credits, provoking more questions than answers.

Andrew Oldham faces all of the above problems and chooses to rely on his own memory for detail, colour and anecdote to transform this oral history into a multi-dimensional portrait, part cultural study, part self-analytical discovery. The work is copyrighted to Clear Entertainment – a subtle nod to Oldham's current immersion in Scientology. When L. Ron Hubbard conjured the Holy Grail of achieving clarity through Dianetics, he promised that the recipient, once 'clear', would be blessed with total recall of every moment of their life. Oldham isn't in that league, but one of the surprises of the book is how well he recalls incidents after so many years of drugs and alcohol abuse.

Of course, Oldham is predominantly sober blooded during his youth, although he seems intent on drinking from the well of sensual experience at every opportunity. His childhood is fascinating and crammed with incident and mystery. A self-absorbed bastard only child, Oldham has no extended family or siblings on whom to model his behaviour. From the age of eight, he seems incorrigibly addicted to glamour, immersing himself in a private fantasy world of movies, music and wish-fulfilling daydreams. His primordial desire is for a life which, in his own words, "didn't end up on the cutting room floor".

One of the great mysteries of the book revolves around his relationship with his mother, an immigrant who keeps her own counsel and responds to her wayward son with a mixture of encouragement and impatience. Seemingly self-assured and occasionally glamorous, Celia Oldham is partly kept by a married man in an affair which is oddly open for the era. Celia even fraternizes with her lover's wife without any sign of friction. Andrew's response to all this is disconcerting. After accidentally seeing his mother and her man friend making love he feigns suicide – complete with a chair and rope suspended from the ceiling. The incident is passed off like a joke, as if the melodramatic Oldham is merely playing the drama queen. Yet as we read on, there are other psychological undertones, with Oldham coyly admitting an adolescent suspicion – mistaken – that his mother was sexually attracted to him. Stranger still are two separate accounts from people who insist that Andrew physically assaulted his mother, incidents for which he confesses to have no recollection. While insisting they must be fabrications rather than painful memories

he has blocked out, his uncertainty on the issue, amid conflicting accounts, leaves the reader questioning the moral framework while realizing that there are no pat answers. This psychological hornet's nest remains unresolved largely because Celia, now sadly diagnosed with Alzheimer's, cannot be interviewed. Either Oldham is in denial, the victim of a Dr Jekyll and Mr Hyde memory loss, or his own myth-making has become part of other people's history to his disadvantage. What comes across most forcibly, both from photographic and anecdotal evidence, is the profound influence of this sometimes remarkable woman on Andrew's world view. Both are portrayed as "ever with an eye on the main chance".

Frighteningly precocious, Oldham is besotted with stardom yet acutely aware that it is manufactured. Barely into his teens, he idolizes Johnnie Ray, obtaining his autograph and wearing a hearing aid in honour of his hero – just like Morrissey later did in the Eighties. When Bill Haley arrives in London, Oldham is again in the audience, now sporting a kiss curl. A rock'n'roll Zelig, he pops up all over the place. Yet he is never entirely consumed by fandom and shows an even greater interest in the architects of fame, paying special attention to producers, managers and behind the scenes players. Barely out of short trousers, he is soon knocking on the door of a neighbourly B-movie actor, desperate to learn the mechanics of show-biz – the gossip, stories and scams. Improbably, the 12-year-old Oldham visits Denmark Street and attempts to sell a song, 'Boomerang Rock' – a crude Tommy Steele cash-in. What is most remarkable here is Oldham's claim that he understood that the real money lay in publishing, a sophisticated perception not shared by most pop stars of the period. Later, he hangs around Tin Pan Alley, regularly attending the 2 I's, star spotting, savouring cappuccinos and living out a self-conscious Fifties myth. There are a handful of parachronisms here, including the dating of the Haley UK show and the 2 I's action appearing in 1956 rather than 1958, but even if Oldham was 14 rather than 12, he still seems outrageously young for such experiences. His novitiate is completed when he sees the stage production of *Expresso Bongo* in 1957: "It became my liturgy: a scenario where the manager was equally important as the artist". One of the great achievements of the book is Oldham's ability to provide authentic snapshots of Fifties' London without lapsing into sociological cliché or Pathé News familiarity. His voice is also strong and evocative, although he occasionally slips into irksome American slang ("pleasured up", "lucked out", "educating up") and usage ("men's room", school "grades"), which sound a little out of place amid the quaint British scenery. It is a rare aberration.

More often, Oldham's use of language is a thing of wonder. He once imitated Anthony Burgess's style in *A Clockwork Orange* but over the years he has honed and refined a conversational and writing voice that is both opaque and intoxicating. Marianne Faithfull remembers being intimidated by the man's "mystifying jive speak", admitting: "I had no idea what he was talking about most of the time". Indeed, his recollections are peppered with fragments of song lyrics, film characters, subtle allusions and evanescent movie dialogue, which is doubly gratifying if you happen to be in the know. At times it's like sharing a secret language. It will baffle those readers with only a passing knowledge of popular culture but presumably Oldham wouldn't want their noses in his book anyway. One of the sentences that perplexed me was the odd: "I'd been cause out of faith in effects". A translation would be appreciated. Fans of Barry McGuire and Bob Dylan will no doubt be relieved to know that "the eve of destruction would be a slow train coming". Elsewhere Oldham offers some brilliant turns of phrase and is the master of the wry one-liner: "I wanted to become Phil Spector not Eric Easton". He is at his best when remembering incidents that caused him a frisson of excitement. His memory of seeing the Beatles for the first time is positively portentous: "The noise that night hit me emotionally, like a blow to the chest. The audience that evening expressed something beyond repressed adolescent sexuality. The noise they made was the sound of the future."

Oldham's tendency to play the method actor is a constant throughout the book. An exhibitionist, he even loses his virginity by his front window with the curtains open, just to annoy the neighbours. His tendency to treat life as a continual performance is reflected in the various tones of voice that emerge in different chapters. At one point, reminiscing about a beatnik girl, he adopts a highly rhetorical romance style like an over-reaching Mills & Boon narrator: "I blushed, her eyes furnaced above the pale mask she wore. My hand wondered how pale was the rest of her, as our arms clasped around each other a little tighter to preserve and bottle the moment. Laughter and love went together and we settled for harmony; we'd both just been and felt effective jazz." The reader, taken aback by this flourish of purple prose, barely has time to ponder the curious adjective "effective" jazz before Oldham switches voices, punctuating his rhapsody with a treatise on French New Wave cinema, Noel Coward, British auteurs, American jazz, Hampstead mores, and a brief history of the English suit.

By the early Sixties, the young Oldham finds himself at the epicentre of the fashion industry, working for Mary Quant and Peter Hope Lumley, while moonlighting at Ronnie Scott's and the Flamingo in the evening and becoming a jazz buff. His contention that the birth of new British fashion filled the gap between Elvis and the Beatles, spearheading fresh attitudes and a *carpe diem* bohemianism, is convincing. Indeed, Oldham's immersion in the rag trade sharpens his vision, ensuring that he appreciates pop culture as a cornucopia of clothes, attitude and music. It is a lesson learned and imitated years later by Malcolm McLaren. Oldham's forays to France also extend his social circle as well as providing dangerous situations in which he can test his nerve and abilities as a loquacious con-man. After begging on the streets, he beats up and robs an "old poof", gets turned on to marijuana by Picasso, ends up in a police cell and is seduced by an older woman while hitchhiking.

After returning to England, Oldham eventually moves into PR, working for the fearsome Don Arden, pop singer Mark Wynter and significantly Brian Epstein. There are tales of encounters with Bob Dylan, John Lennon and Phil Spector, but Oldham is never completely seduced by rock'n'roll royalty. Instead, it's the minor players in the story who rightly receive the plaudits. Although flippant, Oldham is never less than generous to those mentors

who provided his education in the academy of pop. He takes particular care to single out figures such as managers Ray Mackender and Jean Lincoln, whose passion, commitment, humanity and business acumen taught him so much. It's also pleasing to see Oldham championing the often unfairly maligned Dick Rowe, the man singled out by Epstein for turning down the Beatles – a not uncommon occurrence – but whose A&R pedigree was otherwise impressive. Oldham also gives space to less hip singers like Kenny Lynch and Gene Pitney, whose observations are never less than convincing and astute. And who else but Oldham would incorporate the fictional voice of Johnny Jackson, the irresistible, streetwise manager immortalized in *Expresso Bongo*?

After some learned and provocative comments on the state of record production and publishing in the Sixties, Oldham at last turns his attention to the Rolling Stones, approximately half-way through the book. There are many people convinced that, without Oldham's promotional genius, the Stones might never have happened or alternatively would have stalled at the level of the Yardbirds or Pretty Things – respected, but never regarded as cultural icons in the Beatles' class. Oldham is careful not to overstate his case, modestly suggesting: "People say I made the Stones. I didn't. They were there already." For those unkind enough to say he was merely lucky to stumble upon them after a recommendation from *Record Mirror*'s Peter Jones, Oldham counters: "There are no accidents and Peter Jones was the conduit to my destiny ... that's the way God planned it. I met the Rollin' Stones and said 'hello' to the rest of my life."

Oldham cuts an impressive figure when he first encounters the Stones. Although younger than Jagger, he comes across as worldly wise and preternaturally mature for his years. By this point he had fused two of his favourite film characters into an awesome hybrid of hustling muscle: "One enjoyed both the charm of [Laurence] Harvey's Johnny Jackson and the good spark of Tony Curtis's Sydney Falco in *The Sweet Smell Of Success*. Better still, I was free as a bird with no J.J. Hunsecker (Burt Lancaster) to be kowtowed to." Oldham's early memories of the individual Stones prompt some of the best writing in the book. His descriptions of their onstage appeal are particularly illuminating. There's Bill Wyman "stood like a statue who became a celebrity, concentrated, nonchalant, picking his instrument in an upright ... army drill position, perhaps as a result of having seen service as Bill Perks for Queen and country. He was gaunt, pale, almost medieval in a way." Or Charlie Watts: "Unlike the jacketless other five, he had the two top buttons of his jacket done up meticulously over a just as neat button-down shirt and tie, unaffected by the weather in the room. Body behind kit, head turned right in a distant, mannered disdain for the showing of hands waving at 78rpm in front of him. He was with the Stones but not of them, kinda blue, like he'd been transported for the evening from Ronnie Scott's or Birdland, where he'd been driving in another Julian 'Cannonball' Adderley time and space." Keith Richards is the "hollowed cheeked one" who "effected an alchemic exchange in cool hand heat with himself." Finally, Oldham throws in some humorously grotesque imagery, describing Ian Stewart's "Popeye torso" and "William Bendix jaw-

line", Brian Jones's "head having forgone a neck, slipped straight into a subliminally deformed Greystoke body" and Jagger completing the jungle similes as "an adolescent Tarzan".

Beneath the instant mythology, Oldham never loses sense of the harsher aspects of the business. His comments on the psychology of stardom are beyond cynicism: "There's no remorse when they kill, no regrets when they pimp and no shame when they whore". He goes on to recount the familiar rise of the Stones – the Decca deal, BBC appearances, Ian Stewart's removal, the release of 'Come On', the chart fixing, PR scams, and low-key debut album with its grandiloquent assertion, "The Rolling Stones Are More Than Just A Group. They Are A Way Of Life". Oldham expands on several aspects of the Stones' story, revealing co-manager Eric Easton's increasing uneasiness and Brian Jones's incessant scheming. Those overfamiliar with Stones' lore will welcome the revelations about Gene Pitney's attempts to turn Jones into a songwriter and the truth behind minor figures such as George Bean, the first person to cover one of the group's songs.

Of course it is Oldham himself who must take credit for transforming Jagger/Richards into unwilling songwriters, famously locking them in a kitchen until they emerged with the goods. His own work in fashioning the rough 'As Time Goes By' into 'As Tears Go By' for the ingenue Marianne Faithfull also deserves commendation. Given their reverence for the blues and discomfort with the notion of writing songs, the Stones could easily have followed the Animals and found themselves overly dependent upon American tunesmiths. Perhaps bullying them into songwriting was Oldham's most important contribution to the coffers of Jagger/Richards, although he surprisingly makes no comment on the matter beyond the casual observation: "I had this thing that whatever I decided people could be, they became."

Oldham's magnanimity is occasionally countered by some amusing snatches of bitchiness, usually directed at Brian Jones or Mick Jagger. At one point he compares Jagger to his beloved Beagle, Ruby – "Mick and I were as close for awhile as two young men could probably become. These days I enjoy the same with my dog." It may be worth noting that Ruby is seldom, if ever, released from her lead in public. Oldham provides a glimpse into the young Jagger before his persona became overwhelmed with countless masks and a bewildering concoction of different accents. Here he is portrayed as the vulnerable, insecure lover confessing his fears and concerns over his relationship with Chrissie Shrimpton. Jagger has never appeared as unguarded as in these moments. Perhaps this partly explains why he never reconciled with Oldham, even years after their falling out – although that it is a story which is no doubt being saved for a future volume.

Although Oldham remains endearingly idealistic and generous of spirit throughout the book, there is some evidence of expediency and an often present amorality. The heartless firing of Ian Stewart is conducted with the emotional detachment of a dentist extracting a rotten tooth. "Hurt was not in my vocabulary," Oldham admits, adding with hindsight, "but perhaps it should have been". His former wife, Sheila Klein, arguably the most perceptive and revealing speaker in the entire book, provides a dev-astating insight into Oldham's psychological manipulation. "Andrew would test people all the time," she observes, "people would get used up if they couldn't actually match up to his ideal. Like a child, he'd test and test …".". This emotional immaturity at the centre of Oldham's teenage character can probably be traced back to his childhood, when real friends were replaced by film stars and mundane reality was subservient to flights of fantasy. But it should also be stressed that Oldham's mind games were symptomatic of the new cult of youth challenging everything in its path. There are similarly cruel games displayed in written accounts of the early life of John Lennon. Testing people for treachery was also a favoured tactic of Bob Dylan, who drove sycophants and friends to distraction. One of his ploys was to confide imaginary transgressions to colleagues and then wait to hear if they got back to him from a secondary source. In this wilfully immature mind game, Dylan could always convince himself that he was playing God and subsequently banish the transgressor to the ultimate hell – the absence of Dylan. There is something of the same mind set in Oldham, with one speaker suggesting: "He thought he was better than God".

The ever incisive Sheila Klein goes right to the heart of Oldham's psyche, arguing that he was either afraid or incapable of expressing passionate human love at this significant stage of his life. His vampiric, all-consuming hunger for the thrill of it all are summed up in a handful of harrowing sentences: "I wouldn't say he used people, he just used them up. There was nothing left after Andrew went through them, me included. It took me ten years to recover from our relationship; at the end I couldn't actually speak". If Sheila Klein is a victim of Andrew Oldham, then the same can be said of the man himself. He has one fatal flaw. Behind the confidence and energy lies the curse of manic depression, a dark beast that constantly threatens to undo all his achievements.

One fortunate recipient of Oldham's apparently dysfunctional psychology was Mick Jagger, whom Nik Cohn claims "became almost his disciple". Jagger is portrayed as "more of a projection of Andrew than of himself". Certainly, Jagger's chameleon personality and love of role play in the media reflect Oldham's own method acting tactics. The enduring image of Oldham that this book presents is impressively dualistic. On the one hand there is the camp, effete, well-tailored boy/man, sashaying across Soho in make-up with an array of well-connected gay friends. Then there is the other Andrew, playing the part of Don Arden's spiritual heir, running around with the toy gangster Reg The Butcher and frightening enemies in the media and showbusiness with melodramatic displays of threatened violence. As ever Oldham plays the part with uncompromising ease. "He didn't just have arguments with people, he had World Wars," quips former *NME* writer Chris Hutchins. What is not stated here is the ingenious way Mick Jagger assimilated both of Oldham's contrasting images, ultimately fusing them on celluloid in the chilling *Performance*. Now there was a role that Oldham could have played with conviction, if the evidence of this book is accepted.

After 352 pages with no end in sight, Oldham closes his book on an anticlimactic note. The Stones have yet to enjoy their first number 1 with 'It's All Over Now' or undertake their first US tour. Everything of real significance in their story is yet to be written. Like a seasoned stripper Oldham plays the tease, leaving the salivating audience with voyeuristic visions of revelations to come: the Stones' rise to pop glory in 1965 with 'The Last Time'/'Satisfaction'/'Get Off Of My Cloud' triumvirate; the public urination scandal; riotous tours; *Aftermath*; drugs; Redlands; court cases; Oldham's exile from the Stones' camp; the rise and fall of Immediate Records; Allen Klein; Monterey; the distant death of Brian Jones; and Oldham's mysterious abdication of pop godhead.

While turning the final page, my mind commuted back to an early interview with the Mamas & the Papas in *NME* in which a wide-eyed Cass Elliot exclaimed: "He's only 19. Can you imagine what he'll be like when he's 30?" Oldham leaves us pondering the same question as Mama Cass. What we already know from this volume is that Oldham, for all his great hustling adventures, seems more concerned with sensation than profit. Crucially, his ultimate goal appears to be the transformation of event into myth. If this was a work of fiction then Oldham would return in volume 2 as a cross between David Geffen and Richard Branson and take his place as the world's most powerful record baron, swallowing up Decca and EMI Records, buying Oldham Athletic Football Club, founding Oldham Airlines and finally being awarded an autumnal knighthood like those other drug users Paul McCartney and Elton John. In the end, the fictional Oldham could have become a hipper, 21st century version of Sir Joseph Lockwood and Sir Edward Lewis, a corporate J.J.

Hunsecker. The reality is something entirely different. For all his entrepreneurial encounters, Oldham is always more intuitively in touch with the quixotic chancers of *Expresso Bongo* and *The Sweet Smell Of Success* than the high financiers and real power players of the record industry. This is one reason why he spends so much time recreating and reconnecting with that mythical lost world of Fifties London. There lies his personal Eden. As later events will demonstrate, Oldham could happily play Sydney Falco and Johnny Jackson with empathetic ease, but he lacked the cold-blooded, detached ruthlessness to become a J.J. Hunsecker.

As a work in progress, Oldham's odyssey is a great story which, in terms of high drama, should reach far greater heights in volume 2. Whether the psychological insights will prove as profound depends upon whether he will be able to find speakers of the perceptive quality and unflinching frankness of Sheila Klein. Whatever else, the crucial Stones' period (1965-67) should guarantee an even greater public interest in the contents. Like a canny manager, Oldham is already stage-managing this autobiography *cum* oral history to ensure that an epic omnibus edition, perhaps embracing three volumes, will provide his ultimate epitaph.

THE PRODUCERS: A MUSICAL COMEDY

by Peter Doggett

"Q: WILL THERE ever be another Beatles?"

GEOFF EMERICK: "No, because of the way record companies function now; they're purely a money-making machine. When I started, there was more of a focus on artistic considerations. Sometimes it didn't matter if the record made money, as long as the artistic aspect was put to the public.
"You have these manufactured bands like the Spice Girls, and the record companies don't have to spend all their money. At one time, it used to be a career for the artist; that was going to be their livelihood for the rest of their lives, they were going to be an entertainer for 20, 30 years. Things have changed, and it's a shame."

ANYONE WHO clings to the belief that the 50s and 60s were the golden era of rock will be warmed by these accusations from the engineer who cut his teeth alongside George Martin as the Beatles recorded *Sgt. Pepper*, and later produced acclaimed albums by Paul McCartney (*Band On The Run*) and Elvis Costello (*Imperial Bedroom*) among many others.

Emerick's jaundiced view of the contemporary record business will be echoed by many of those who feel that rock music lost its soul sometime in the last three decades, but who disagree about the identity of the thief – with punk, rap; MTV and make-up for men among the main suspects.

In Howard Massey's *Behind The Glass*, 37 producers of varying degrees of fame (Emerick among them) are interviewed

about their craft; and their conversations illuminate more than they realise both the current state of the music business, and the shift in technique and philosophy from the 60s to the dawn of the 21st century. The subjects range from legends like George Martin and Brian Wilson, through small-print doyens like Jack Douglas, Tony Visconti and Chic's Nile Rodgers, to relative unknowns (at least in Britain) – Sylvia Massy Shivy, for instance, who proudly produced Tool's album *Undertow* (no, me neither), and Mike Clink (whose credits, if that's the correct word under the circumstances, include Sammy Hagar, Triumph and Survivor).

For anyone not actively considering a career in production, Massey's book is as frustrating as it is enlightening. A practising engineer and producer himself, his questions often lean towards the bewilderingly technical, and bypass the curiosity of the general reader. It takes a particularly narrow mind-set, for example, to interview Eddie Kramer, and scarcely allow him to comment on the pioneering recordings he made in the late 60s with Jimi Hendrix – the work which remains Kramer's chief claim to recognition.

Yet despite his preference for discussing the merits of rival microphones and the minutiae of sampling technique, Massey almost accidentally reveals the ways in which production, and recorded music, have changed over the last four decades.

Proponents of the Geoff Emerick conspiracy theory – crudely, that the early years of rock'n'roll were filled with fun, love of experimentation and artistic integrity, qualities which have been sacrificed to the almighty dollar and the computer chip – will have their prejudices confirmed when they compare the words of Beatles producer George Martin with, for example, Steve Levine, who supervised the Culture Club phenomenon in the 80s.

No matter how well-worn they may be, Martin's anecdotes of life with 'the four boys' at Abbey Road can be instantly understood by anyone who has heard the records. For perhaps the 5000th time, he describes how he and the Beatles threw small fragments of taped fairground music into the air, then reassembled them entirely at random. Play 'Being For The Benefit Of Mr. Kite' on *Sgt. Pepper*, and you can hear the results – exactly what you'd expect from this musical version of William Burroughs' cut-up technique.

Levine's dialogue, however, is altogether more mystifying. Asked how he approaches the task of mixing a record, he muses: "Especially with digital desks, you have to listen as you EQ ... You have to mix and match, filter a few things, put a few things through a synth, use different EQs just for the sake of it, run signals through different pieces of outboard gear in bypass mode ... Changing the phase relationships can make a huge difference." Come again, Steve? "Putting the drum overheads through outboard boxes can help separate the drum kit, even if you don't add much EQ." And so on and on: without a degree in record production (coming to your local university soon), it's virtually impossible to fathom a word that Levine is saying, let alone imagine how his methods might influence the sound of his records.

While the language of production has mutated beyond recognition, those at the other end of the musical process – the songwriters – can still discuss their work in terms that would be familiar to their ancestors. For proof, consult Paul Zollo's superb *Songwriters On Songwriting* (Da Capo Press, £14.95), a weighty collection of interviews with craftsmen and women as diverse as Bob Dylan and Yoko Ono, Willie Dixon and k.d. lang. Although their songs shared little beyond the common language of music, Sammy Cahn (lyricist for many Sinatra classics) and Madonna would have had no difficulty in relating to each other. "It's like free association. I'll start singing words (to a melody) and making them fit." And again: "When I listen to a melody I hear words ... Lyrics sing to the ear, the mind, the heart." (The first quote is Madonna, the second Cahn.)

While Zollo's songwriters talk in similar conceptual terms across the decades, Masser's producers are divided not just by age and technical expertise, but philosophy. The relatively simplistic equipment available to George Martin in 1966 forced him to become a father of invention when John Lennon wanted 'Tomorrow Never Knows' to sound as if it were being sung by a thousand Buddhist monks on a mountain-top. Steve Levine probably already has that very sound programmed into his sampler.

So Karl Marx might have been right when he declared that changing economic conditions inexorably altered the means of production (though he could never have imagined *Sgt. Pepper*, let alone Sammy Hagar). Thereafter the traditionalists' argument unrolls itself. Producers and musicians have lost the ability to transform sound by using their hands to alter the way it is recorded; instead, all these changes and innovations are carried out by extremely sophisticated machines. Hence music has lost its personality and its soul to the computer, the sampler and the dreaded Fairlight keyboard. When George Martin oversaw the Beatles' most ambitious recordings, there was literally no division of labour between the producer and the artist. In the modern age, the computer intervenes between the human participants at every stage of the process. Case closed.

Except ... the producers refuse to divide themselves neatly into rival camps. Key personnel from each era are traded like spies at the border; more confusingly, some of Massey's interviewees are plainly double agents, working for both sides.

Enter Walter Afanasieff, who should be the chief witness for the prosecution. His sins include Mariah Carey, Michael Bolton, Kenny G, Savage Garden and (completing the cast of the Evil Empire) Celine Dion. His philosophy is total domination of the artist, and subjugation to the

machine. "Technology", he admits vaguely, "sort of prevails in my life." And his ideal sound could serve as piped music for the inner circle of hell: "I like big drums. I like really big background vocals. I like huge rock guitars, even if it's a really light R&B song." Yet Afanasieff's avowed role models are the holy trinity of 60s traditionalists: the Beatles, George Martin, and the Beach Boys' *Pet Sounds*.

Enter Glen Ballard, co-creator of Alanis Morissette's *Jagged Little Pill*, and sonic server for 90s AOR acts from Wilson Phillips to the Corrs. He concedes that "with the technology available to us now, it's very easy to ... postpone any kind of decision-making, because you can literally record as many takes as you want and keep everything. Secondly, you can obviously clean up everything. You can tune [up] vocals, you can time-adjust everything – you can really make it all perfect on paper." Ideal ammunition for the man who made a singer out of dancer Paula Abdul, you might think. But Ballard's stated intent is to subvert the domination of his technology, and seek out "immediacy" and a "visceral connection with the music". Even Geoff Emerick couldn't argue with that.

The veterans are no more predictable. Tony Visconti, who produced Bolan and Bowie's finest 70s work, proudly claims new technology as "another tool in my arsenal", and opines that "you have to be an artist ... how you record is irrelevant". Brian Wilson (who says that "you know when you're through eating, and you know when you're through producing"; no jokes, please, about his frequent obesity) reckons that the computer "really helps in the production ... you have much more control over the overall sound".

And it's Nile Rodgers, the producer of *Let's Dance*, perhaps David Bowie's most clinical album, but also of Chic's irrepressibly vibrant series of disco albums, who finally erases the boundary line between the generations. In perhaps the most enlightening conversation in Massey's book, Rodgers is asked whether he thinks records sound better today than they did 20 years ago. "Absolutely not," he replies. "Because whatever we've gained in technical superiority, it makes us not necessarily work as hard ... The old restrictions in technology forced us to do things right. It forced us to make decisions. It forced us to spiritually be so in tune with the other people that magic had to happen ... There was no way that you they could fix it and make it better."

Yet Rodgers admits that some aspects of technology are impossible to fault: "We can do so much now that we used to have to toil over in the old days, and now I can't really tell the difference, especially spiritually."

'Spiritually' – that's not a word used by Walter Afanasieff or George Martin, and if it occurs in Brian Wilson's conversation, it has more to do with the complex workings of his psyche than his musical philosophy ("my soul feels a little weird sometimes, so I need music to help it out"). But however you define the term, 'spiritually' is as evocative as any description of the way we experience the most powerful rock music, whether that be Elvis Presley in 1954, the Sex Pistols in 1977, or Radiohead in 2001. Nile Rodgers suggests that technology has not replaced soulfulness in the producer's palette, but merely distracted it. The art is not to enslave yourself to the computer, or pretend that it was never existed, but to twist it to your own ends.

In the 60s, musical purists complained that pop wasn't real music because it depended on electricity (older readers will remember the jibes about the Beatles being silenced if there were a power cut). Although Howard Massey's book can be cited to prove a dozen conflicting theories, its most persuasive prose testifies that 21st century recording technology is like electricity: it can take away life, or transform it.

DOUBLE ACT
GREIL MARCUS, BILL CLINTON AND ELVIS

FETED BY many as America's most distinguished rock critic, Greil Marcus has also been criticised in recent years for squeezing the music to fit his theories – particularly in *Invisible Republic*, his thought-provoking but at times tenuous book (loosely) about Bob Dylan's *Basement Tapes*.

Advance warning of *Double Trouble: Bill Clinton And Elvis Presley In A Land Of No Alternatives* (Faber & Faber, £9.99) triggered much amusement from the sceptical, who wondered if Marcus could really carry off his comparison between two slightly overweight Southern enigmas who flirted with destroying their cultural power by their excessive behaviour inside their mansions.

The reality was something less, and yet more, than that. *Double Trouble* proved to be a provocative collection of essays – "some about Elvis," as Marcus conceded, "some about Clinton, some about the symbiosis of the two and some mentioning neither". But it was prefaced by an essay which teased out all the implications of that comparison in convincing style. (The fact that members of the Bush cabinet have already begun comparing their man to Elvis will no doubt trigger another Marcus book.)

Until then, which British critic will have the courage to pen our own *Double Trouble*? For if Bill Clinton is the Elvis Presley of American politics, then surely Tony Blair is our Cliff Richard – a moralistic conservative wearing the regalia of a creed that was once a call to revolution, and is now merely a tame parody. Just as Marcus might imagine Clinton joining Elvis for a midnight jam on 'Heartbreak Hotel', is it too far-fetched to conceive Tony Blair mildly strutting his stuff alongside Sir Cliff at some charity bash, trusty Fender in hand, lovingly crooning 'Living Doll' while Cherie grimaces with anguished embarrassment in the front row?

THE SONG IS OVER

THE SONG is dead, say a generation of aficionados raised on the work of Rodgers & Hart, Gershwin, Porter, Lennon & McCartney, Bacharach & David, even Lloyd Webber. Disc jockey Mike Read obviously agrees, although his disappointingly lightweight *The Death Of Songwriting* is better at explaining what's vanished than what forced its departure.

So it's almost a shock to turn the glossy, large-format pages of Spencer Leigh's *Brother, Can You Spare A Rhyme? 100 Years Of Hit Songwriting* (Spencer Leigh Ltd., £16.99), and become lost in a world where 16th century hits such as 'Greensleeves' (for which Henry VIII, not content with marrying half the country's women, also grabbed all the writing credit) and 'Gaudete' are seen in the same tradition as 'Candle In The Wind', 'Common People' and indeed 'Living La Vida Loca'.

The key word in Leigh's title is 'hit', and his book – a fascinating assemblage of pop trivia from throughout the 20th century, plus interviews with writers like Jimmy Webb, Elvis Costello, the late Sammy Cahn and Sir Tim Rice – destroys all musical classifications based on genre and *NME* appeal. It also deconstructs the precise balance of the Lennon/McCartney partnership, concluding that the Lennon estate owes Sir Paul a sizeable royalty cheque.

Most valuable is its detailed research into the history of songs that have survived the century – not just modern pop classics such as 'My Way' and 'American Pie', but right back to the early 1900s and such familiar titles as 'Land Of Hope And Glory', 'We Shall Overcome' and 'O Sole Mio' (alias 'It's Now Or Never', or if you prefer, the Cornetto ad).

With his ears open to every form of mainstream (that is, 'hit') songwriting, Leigh's book is a throwback to 60s titles like *The Daily Mail Book Of Golden Discs* by Joseph Murrels, which likewise saw no distinction between high opera and low novelty culture. *Brother, Can You Spare A Rhyme?* mightn't attract cult status, but its expansive landscape is truer to the century that has just passed than any sharply focused study of hip-hop or (dare I say?) country rock.

LE JOUR DE GLOIRE EST ARRIVÉ
L'HISTOIRE DE SERGE GAINSBOURG

by Peter Doggett

"HE HAD a typical French feel for rock," wrote *The Guardian* after the death of Serge Gainsbourg. "He was hopeless at it." That quote appears early in both the English-language biographies of Gainsbourg, the second of which – Sylvie Simmons' witty and perceptive *Serge Gainsbourg: A Fistful Of Gitanes* (Helter Skelter, £12.99) – is just published.

Until Air began soundtracking Hollywood movies, and Gainsbourg's minimalist masterpiece *L'Histoire De Melodie Nelson* album entered the mainstream as a cult favourite in the late 90s, most enquiring rock minds had usually been exposed to just one piece of French pop. And that was 'Je T'Aime', Gainsbourg and Jane Birkin's beautiful but almost hilariously restrained evocation of sexual ecstasy, which evoked a national scandal when it was released here in 1969.

In an era when adult music listeners readily discuss their favourite Cuban piano-players, or debate the merits of dance music from Mali and Mozambique, it is peculiar (or a testament to the width of the *English* Channel) that we have taken so little interest in the distinctive pop tradition rooted 25 miles off our shores.

Occasional attempts have been made to smuggle French talent across the border. Françoise Hardy briefly emerged as a hybrid of Sandie Shaw and Donovan in the mid-60s, though her success in Britain seems to have owed more to her film star looks than to any appreciation of her work. Charles Aznavour made a lightning raid on British hearts in the 70s with 'She'. But beyond a vague suspicion that France's most famous pop star, Johnny Hallyday, probably sounds like Cliff Richard crossed with Pat Boone, our defences have remained resolutely unbroken by

Francophone popular music ever since.

The case for mutual understanding probably isn't aided by the knowledge that the first wave of French rock'n'roll, in the late 50s, was dubbed *yaourt* (or 'yoghurt'), because that's how the rebel yell sounded to French ears. Nor does the Parisian infatuation with *le twist* endear us to the prospect of soaking in the French Top 40.

Yet beneath the insipid dance tunes and maudlin ballads, France has bred an underground strain of inspired and sometimes chaotically eclectic talents. Antoine was their closest equivalent to mid-60s Bob Dylan; his back-up band, the Problems, were once memorably described by pop archivist Kieron Tyler as sounding "like the Pretty Things falling downstairs". The pure pop concoctions of Sylvie Vartan and France Gall (much of whose work was penned by Serge Gainsbourg) are a match for Britain's own 60s pop 'girls'; while Ronnie Bird's snarling R&B is a more than respectable response to the Stones' existential angst.

And then there are Jacques Dutronc and Michel Polnareff, both of whom elude facile comparisons. Dutronc emerged as a blues-inspired Donovan, and mutated into a film star, a satirist and a pop auteur of some class. Even more magnificently, Polnareff created a series of ambitious and sonically bizarre late 60s and early 70s pop gems, the best of which place him alongside Jimmy Webb, Brian Wilson, Lou Christie and Gene Pitney in the company of art-pop dramatists.

All of those cultural terrorists and pop subversives pale, however, alongside Gainsbourg – whose almost unfathomable recording career encompassed cocktail jazz, Anglophile pop, French reggae, deathly black humour, satire, romance, erotic compulsion, despair, traditional chansons, avant-garde rock, rap, mid-60s experiments in African percussion, and a verbal dexterity and panache that, Dylan aside, is unmatched by anyone working in the Anglo-American pop tradition.

The publication of Alan Clayson's biography of Gainsbourg in 1998 allowed his work slowly to infiltrate British culture; Sylvie Simmons' eminently readable book should speed that process into a stampede. As she admits, the project had humble journalistic beginnings: "When *Mojo* started their Cult Heroes series, I suggested doing a piece on Serge. What was commissioned as a 500-word feature turned into quite a large *Mojo* feature, and then into a much larger book!" Though she admits that she was only familiar with a couple of Gainsbourg records when she began her research – the *Histoire De Melodie Nelson* album and the inevitable 'Je T'Aime' – she had been long been fascinated by this enigmatic figure who meant so much in France and so little on this side of la Manche.

"I spent almost three years living in the South-West of France in the early 90s," Simmons says. "I had been there about six months when Serge died [in March 1991], and what struck me was the effect that his death had on the people that I knew – everyone from a young hip academic, to a neighbour who was in his 70s. That was when I realised that he was more than just a controversial celebrity or a pop singer."

The apparently insuperable language barrier that emphasises the centuries-old suspicion between Britain and France is accentuated by Gainsbourg's subtle use of assonance and wordplay. "Even though I can speak French," Simmons admits, "I still found it very hard to pick up on all the nuances of Serge's work at first listen. It doesn't translate at all easily into English, because there are often several layers of puns, and other nuances – his use of percussive sounds for words, for instance – which it's almost impossible to reproduce in another language."

Equally forbidding is the difficulty of translating Gainsbourg's cultural and artistic status: "I found it hard to describe Serge to anyone who hadn't been raised in French culture, because there are no obvious equivalents. He's not just a songwriter, or a performer, or an actor, or a satirist, or a celebrity who goes on TV and deliberately shocks his audience. He's all of those things, and much more."

After decades in which he was only known in Britain as one of the protagonists of 'Je T'Aime', Gainsbourg's profile was lifted and twisted in the 90s when a brief Channel 4 documentary first broadcast the footage of an apparently drunken Serge confronting Whitney Houston on a French TV chat show with a delicate mating call: "I want to *fuck* you". Simmons explains that this wasn't the act of an inebriated boor, but a deliberate piece of cultural anarchy: "The whole incident was an absolute thigh-slapper, if you understand how it happened. You have to see it in the context of these appalling variety and chat shows that they still have on French TV, as if nothing has changed since the 50s. They usually feature middle-aged celebrities, passing round a hand-held mike and telling each other how much they admire each other. It just happened that Whitney Houston's promotional schedule landed her on one of these shows, but it was a nauseating programme, and it needed something like that to happen."

The incident was reminiscent of one of those equally outlandish UK chat show appearances made by Oliver Reed at the height of his own alcohol-fuelled notoriety – when even his friends weren't quite sure of the dividing-line between acting and intoxication. Simmons is happy to admit the similarity: "There certainly was something of the same spirit in Serge as in Oliver Reed. So maybe a way to begin to describe Serge would be as a bizarre combination of Elvis Presley, except that he wrote his own songs; Johnny Rotten, except that he wasn't a punk; and Oliver Reed. But that still only captures a portion of his personality, and his work."

A paragraph from Simmons' book comes close to evoking the ambiguity of his persona: "A 'double agent' is how French newspaper *Liberation* once described Serge and it's an appellation that's hard to argue with. A master of duality, he wrote disposable pop and classic chansons, songs about love and songs about shit, quoted trash American TV and movies with the same zeal and acuity as he did Baudelaire, Verlaine and Prévert." The ambivalence doesn't end there: forced to wear the Jewish star by the Nazis during the war, Gainsbourg later devoted an entire album not to a memorial for the six million massacred, but to a Mel Brooks-style rock'n'roll evocation of life with the Adolf Hitlers, *Rock Around The Bunker*. A devoted father, he recorded duets about incest with his daughter Charlotte. Equally besotted with his long-time companion, Jane Birkin, he conceived a movie in which she would be anally gang-raped. Artistic confrontation was not a pose for Gainsbourg, but a way of life.

Simmons conducted a series of lengthy interviews with Birkin for her book, and the actress's memories and insights are perhaps its strongest asset. "Jane has been reticent to talk about Serge in the past," Simmons notes, "but her motivation in talking to me was that she said when he was alive, he very much wanted approval for his work in Britain. He couldn't understand why he wasn't better known here. So she was delighted to do anything now that might alter that situation."

Birkin also provides a brief, poetic and oblique introduction to the book. In person, she is apparently no more direct: "Jane has a very fast way of talking, which is almost stream of consciousness, and no matter where you begin a conversation, she can cover almost any subject along the way. She has total recall, but it sometimes takes you quite a long time to get the answer to your original question."

Although Birkin didn't meet Gainsbourg until the late 60s, she was able to provide Simmons with information about every area of his life – including the anecdote which inspires the book's dramatic opening line: "Serge Gainsbourg owed his life to dirt". Indeed, she is sometimes able to puncture his own hyperbole, revealing that Gainsbourg's family had been able to correct some of his more exaggerated statements about his upbringing and early life.

Serge's refusal to separate his artistic and personal lives, and to treat his media encounters as creative statements, suggests that although Simmons regrets not being able to speak to him before his death, his testimony might have added as many distractions as revelations to her story.

Birkin's reflective and sometimes regretful testimony (plus that of Gainsbourg's producer, Philippe Lerichomme) adds a dimension to this book which sadly wasn't available to Gainsbourg's previous bio-grapher, Alan Clayson. His aptly-titled *View From The Exterior* (Sanctuary, 1998; £12.99) provided more cultural context than Simmons' account but less personal insight.

The books also differ in their perception of Gainsbourg's artistic milieu. Clayson quite rightly emphasised the singer's debt to, and reaction against, the rich *chansons* tradition in France; Simmons, as she admits, "saw the *chansons* period as a fascinating step that he took on the road to becoming a pop genius".

Forced to examine the scenery as well as the road by his lack of first-hand interview material, Clayson's book concentrated on bringing alive not just the man but the culture (in the widest sense) from which he came. Without ever examining her prey in a vacuum, Simmons still focuses much more tightly on Gainsbourg himself. Her book also has the advantage of more overt humour (although the sly irony of Clayson's account shouldn't be discounted). She illuminates her portrait with colourful flashes of description, noting in her introduction, for example, that "Serge looked like an elegant turtle cross-bred with a particularly louche, chain-smoking wolf".

Lighter, breezier and more accessible, Simmons' book is more likely than Clayson's to entice the mildly intrigued observer into Gainsbourg's unnerving and outlandish world. It captures its audience with material where it already feels comfortable (the outrage, the sex, the inevitable smouldering Gitanes) and then drags them gently to the heart of the beautiful monster that was Gainsbourg's art. But Clayson's portrait, and his wider commentary on French popular culture, should not be dismissed. What's required now (in France as much as in Britain) is an intelligent and opinionated history of French pop that will open up its treasures to the perennially suspicious British audience. Then all that's left is to ensure that everyone in Britain speaks perfect French. Oh, well: back to *la planche à dessin*.

NECESSITY IS:
DON PRESTON OF THE MOTHERS OF INVENTION

BILLY JAMES has recently published his book of reminiscences by the original members of Frank Zappa's Mothers of Invention. For *Necessity Is...* (SAF Publishing), Billy talked to many of the ex-members of Zappa's first, and arguably best, band. In a revealing and often humorous book, Jimmy Carl Black, Bunk Gardner, Motorhead Sherwood, Buzz Gardner, Roy Estrada and Dick Kunc recount their experiences working and touring with Frank in the sixties. Another major contributor is the redoubtable Don Preston. Preston is well known for his work in the Jazz world as well as the score for *Apocalypse Now*. We caught up with Don, to talk about Zappa and the book.

What do you think about the book – Necessity Is...The Early Years Of Frank Zappa's Mothers Of Invention?

The book represents many of the unusual events that transpired with the Mothers, and it gives deep insights into the individual characteristics of the people who were in the band. It also sheds some light on the relationships between the band members themselves, as well as the relationships between them and Frank Zappa.

In many ways the book is like a family album. Memories of a rock and roll group that broke new ground, set new precedents and shook the fabric of the rock world as it existed then. It was a magic group at a magic time who were brought together by a magic force. *Necessity Is* tells the story...

Do you have a favourite memory of Frank Zappa?

A number of years before the Mothers of Invention, I used to have jam sessions in my garage, in which we would improvise to films of microscopic life, and other art films. And Zappa used to come down, and sit in with us, and be part of the improvisations. Also, sometimes he would bring his own films to the sessions, and we would improvise to them. At the time, he was working with 8mm, and he was doing some very unusual film work. So that was my favourite time with Frank Zappa.

What are you up to these days?
Well, both Bunk Gardner and I are featured on the new ANT-BEE CD, *Electronic Church Muzik*. I was recently nominated for 'Eminent Jazz Musician Of The Year.' Also, I just recorded a CD with my trio, which features me on piano, Alex Cline on drums, and Joel Hamilton on bass. The CD will be released soon. Right now, the Grandmothers recently completed a 2 and a half month tour of the US. The tour covered 14,000 miles of the United States – the first time the Grandmothers had toured America in close to 20 years!

The Grandmothers continue to tour and promote the kind of music and oddball humour that were a trademark of Zappa's entourage between 1964 and 1970. *Necessity Is...* is available now through Helter Skelter, priced £12.99.

PEARLS BEFORE SWINE:
CULT HEROES

FOR MORE than a decade, between the first coming of Madonna and the mutation of her 'material girl' ethos into the Spice Girls, rock publishing was unashamedly dominated by overnight celebrities. No sooner had the Jesus & Mary Chain or Mel & Kim reached the Top 40 than some penniless hack had rewritten their press cuttings, boasting that they were offering "an in-depth biography".

In this world of *Heat, OK!* and fatuous TV 'showbiz' reporting, our desperate desire to consume ever more 'exclusives' about our celebrities now has to be given instant gratification. This has cleared the bookstores for more récherché adventures in rock biography, focusing on subjects who never came close to orthodox stardom.

Mark Brend's *American Troubadours: Groundbreaking Singer Songwriters Of The 60s* (Backbeat Books, £12.95) typifies these obscure quests. It ignores the truly "groundbreaking" talents of the era (Bob Dylan, Joni Mitchell, Paul Simon, Kris Kristofferson) in favour of nine men who have, in the author's eyes, been sidelined by history. Brend's succinct accounts of the careers and turbulent lives of such cult heroes as David Blue, Tim Hardin and David Ackles explore territory which has previously only been touched by rock history magazines, and then rarely in such depth. Beautifully packaged, his book seems to revive the era when record labels such as Elektra would sink hundreds of thousands of dollars into deserving artists who were never likely to repay that investment.

If Brend adopts the role of clear-eyed chronicler, correcting the omissions of the past, Adam Webb treats the rewriting of history as a desperate crusade. *Dumb Angel: The Life And Music Of Dennis Wilson* (Creation Books, £11.95) is the second book about the self-destructive Beach Boys drummer, whose occasional forays into songwriting achieved an epic splendour rivalled only by his elder brother, Brian Wilson. Excessive, opinionated, obsessively detailed, Webb's book is as passionate as the man it chronicles.

More than that, his introduction is a trial and execution of contemporary rock culture, which might revive some very recent memories: "What Rock'n'Roll is now is the soundtrack to the mainstream. A corporate circus. Choreography. So safe and without danger that our leaders get elected to it."

MILES DAVIS:
KIND OF TWO

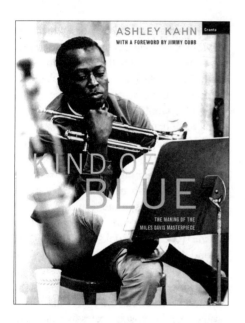

THE SECRET dread of every non-fiction author is that his or her years of research and writing will be punctured by a rival account of exactly the same subject. Anyone tangling with a well-heralded event such as the Millennium, or an anniversary – 500 years since Columbus sailed the ocean blue, 25 since the Pistols swore at Bill Grundy – must anticipate competition. But sometimes a collision of texts simply arises from coincidence, with two writers unknowingly pursuing the same idea.

Recent months have seen the appearance of two books which, from their titles, threatened to be virtually identical: Ashley Kahn's *Kind Of Blue: The Making Of The Miles Davis Masterpiece* (Granta, £20); and Eric Nisenson's *The Making Of Kind Of Blue: Miles Davis And His Masterpiece* (St. Martin's Press, £16.99). Kahn is a rock and jazz journalist and TV editor, who was given unique access to the original session tapes for Miles Davis's unchallenged 1959 gem; Nisenson is the author of the heretical *Blue: The Murder Of Jazz*, plus books about Davis, John Coltrane and Sonny Rollins.

Understandably, many reviewers have considered the two books in opposition, and almost without exception they have lauded Kahn at Nisenson's expense. From its rich pictorial coverage to its smooth prose, there is no doubt that Kahn offers the more accessible artefact; Nisenson's book contains no illustrations, and occasionally the writing jars the ear. Factor in Kahn's revealing account of the recording sessions, and you might decide to call 'no contest'.

But the subtitles of the two books suggest a subtle difference in style which makes them complementary rather than antagonistic. Kahn offers a fluid history of Davis's previous career, and then concentrates, as the title suggests, on the making of the album. By contrast, Nisenson offers a different definition of "making" – gestation, not creation. In his book, several distinct stories meet at the 1959 sessions, with each of the participants bringing his own history to the table, and the exotic jazz philosopher/composer George Russell, who didn't play on the album, leaving his brand on those who did. Kahn treats art as inevitable, Nisenson as the result of a prolonged creative struggle. Kahn shows how *Kind Of Blue* was made; Nisenson reveals how it was *able* to be made.

LENNON REMEMBERS – AGAIN

An Alternative Universe

AFTER BEING seriously injured when he was shot by a crazed fan in December 1980, John Lennon retired from public life. He separated from his wife Yoko Ono, in 1981, although he retained her services as his business manager. Despite years of friendly persuasion from the other Beatles, Lennon chose to take no active part in the giant *Anthology* project, preferring to let his younger self speak on his behalf.

Last December, a flurry of books was published to mark the 20th anniversary of his final musical activity. Rolling Stone publisher Jann Wenner reissued *Lennon Remembers* (Verso, £13), which contains the full text of Lennon's interviews with the magazine in December 1970. David Sheff's *Last Interview* (Sidgwick & Jackson, £9.99) was a reprint of the equally lengthy conversations taped for *Playboy* magazine in 1980. And two other books, Robert Rosen's *Nowhere Man* (Soft Skull, £14.99) and Geoffrey Giuliano's *Lennon In America* (Robson Books, £16.95), competed to provide a definitive account of the former Beatle's final decade in the public eye, both claiming to be based on access to his unpublished diaries.

We approached Yoko Ono for an interview, hoping to discuss the portrayal of her ex-husband in these books. That request was politely declined, but the Lennon office unexpectedly phoned back, promising that "someone else will speak to you soon". Late one night, we received a call from an unmistakeable voice who refused to explain his whereabouts or his motives, but simply said, "Ask me about the books, until I get bored." This is the conversation that ensued.

Why didn't you take part in the Beatles' Anthology?
Jesus. (*long pause*) Twenty years away, and you still want to hear about the Beatles? Read the book, you know, it's all in there.

Have you read it?
Why should I read it? It was bad enough living through it once, without having to rake through all that garbage again. It still bores me, all that Beatles talk.

They were always trying to get me to take part in that movie, even before the shooting. They kept saying that I'd never have to talk about it again, that this would be the last time. But I knew it would just be the beginning. We'd get together in front of the cameras, at Apple or in Paul's house, probably, and then there'd be all this pressure to play, and then Sid Bernstein would be on the fucking phone, begging us to do one more show to save the planet.

You know, Paul wanted me to play at Live Aid. He said that the boys should get together to feed the starving. It's like when we were on tour, and Neil and Mal would have to throw all these cripples out of the dressing-room. They'd be lined up, staring at us, as if we could fucking heal them. Like I used to say to Yoko, we couldn't even heal ourselves, let alone start curing other people.

Paul even gave Geldof the number, the bastard. I had to change it, because he kept phoning every night, begging me to think of the children. I could see them on TV, and I knew that if we gave them food this week, they'd only be starving next week instead. It's a fucking waste of time. Eventually I told him to get Elvis Costello to sing one of my songs, and that I'd be there with him in spirit. That would be my conceptual contribution – like one of Yoko's things from *Grapefruit*, "Imagine he's there, and he will be". And it worked. Geldof left me alone after that.

Why Elvis Costello?

Because I liked what I'd heard, that song about Oswald Mosley and the one about Chelsea. I hadn't studied him, but I knew he was from Liverpool, and he had the Buddy Holly glasses, like I did at art college. So I thought he might be alright. But I had to laugh. What did he sing? 'All You Need Is Love'. Great news if you're starving, Elvis, or whatever your real name is. And it went to his head, being anointed a surrogate Beatle for the afternoon. The next thing I knew, he was writing songs with Paul. After that, I kept waiting for him to marry Yoko.

Couldn't you have stopped the others from making the Anthology films?

I could have, but what was the point? I didn't care if it happened or not, so I told Yoko to give them what they wanted, and then keep out of the way. Neil told me that she was pissed off because they wouldn't give her equal time on camera *in loco parentis*, or whatever it is, to speak on my behalf. But I didn't need anyone to speak for me. I knew the others could talk themselves into fucking trouble without my help.

I wasn't surprised at Paul wanting to do it. He probably had an album he wanted to sell, or some fucking movie. He always had his eye out for an opportunity to sell himself. And I knew Ringo would go along with it, just to keep busy. But I was surprised that George was along for the ride. I thought he had more important things on his mind. He's always talking about enlightenment and nirvana and all that shit, and there he is on TV squabbling about whether or not he helped me write some song on acid in 1965. Why does he care?

It's all so long ago, and none of us can remember anything. We need other people to tell us what happened so we can tell them the stories back. That's why I didn't want to do it. If you want to know what was going on, look at the newsreels and play the records. My songs were always a diary, anyway. If I was having an affair with a chick on tour, there's probably a song about it, like 'Girl' or 'Norwegian Wood' or whatever.

Why did you hand over the tapes of 'Free As A Bird' and 'Real Love' for the others to overdub?

To get them off my backs. I didn't want to be Lennon the spoilsport, stopping the boys from having their fun. So I said I'd send them some songs, and they could pretend I was lying in bed for a week, and they had to finish them off. They'd done that enough times, anyway, in the 60s. After I met Yoko, I was never there. They were used to making records without me. I used to phone up, and if it was time to cut one of George's songs, I'd get Yoko to stage some event, or we'd cut our hair off for peace, or some fucking thing, to give me an excuse not to turn up.

Yoko sent me over a batch of my old tapes, and I starting playing all these songs that weren't even good enough for *Double Fantasy*, if you can believe that. And I was getting so depressed, listening to this guy whining about being lonely and miserable in his luxury apartment on Central Park West. So I thought, fuck them, I'll send them some real shit, and see what they make of it. 'Free As A Bird' was a lame piece of crap, which I'd never finished, or even fucking wanted to finish. It was badly recorded, it was out of time, it was all over the place. And they were so desperate, the boys, so desperate for any fucking fragment of the holy cross, that they spent months slaving over that cassette tape that I'd thrown in a drawer and tried to forget.

What did you think of the finished record?
It wasn't bad, you know, but it wasn't the Beatles. Because I wasn't there. I wasn't in the studio, and I wasn't even there on the fucking tape. I was bored and stoned in the Dakota, and it could have been anyone. But they were always good boys when it came to work. That's why I never felt guilty about skipping school when I met Yoko. I knew that Paul would do my homework for me. He always wanted to be fucking Head Boy.

Did you object to Jann Wenner reissuing the Rolling Stone *interview again?*
I couldn't stop it, so I didn't worry about it. Everyone's already read it, anyway. I was fucking furious the first time, when he put it out as a book. *Rolling Stone* was always a piece of garbage, a *Daily Telegraph* for hippies or whatever it was, but I liked Wenner when I first met him, because he was arrogant and pushy and he reminded me of me. So I did that interview and it kept the paper alive … no, which one was that?

You were interviewed in the first issue of Rolling Stone *in 1967, but the book is from 1970, when you were promoting the* Plastic Ono Band *albums.*
Oh, right. Well, whichever one it was, it was still a fucking favour too far. Wenner looked like a hippie, but he was another one like Richard Branson, where I should have known from the start that he was just another capitalist in a tie-dye shirt. And he proved it with that book. I spent a day or two with him and Yoko in New York, and we went to the movies, and I gave him that interview, or several interviews, and he promised that he'd use it in the magazine. Three months later, it's a fucking book! We tried to stop it, but it was too late. We were already in court for half our lives as it was, so we let the bastard go.

That interview probably did as much to destroy the Beatles' myth as anything. Do you regret being so aggressive towards Paul, George and Ringo, and the guys who worked for you, like Derek Taylor and Neil Aspinall?
I don't even remember what I said. I was stoned out of my head. I'd been through Primal Scream with Janov, and I was still

fucking primalling. It was like when I used to get drunk in Liverpool, and I'd come round when I was beating up some sailor, or attacking Bob Wooler with a cricket bat, like I did at Paul's 21st. All this fucking bile would come pouring out, like that girl in *The Exorcist*, and I had no control.

We'd been out of Janov's therapy for about six months, and it was supposed to free you of all the past shit that was weighing you down. Instead, I couldn't breathe without thinking about the past. The pain of it was incredible. It was all my mother, and Mimi, and Stu Sutcliffe, and my fucking daddy abandoning me, and Epstein, and all that shit, day after day. I couldn't deal with it, so I went back on H. Then Wenner came along and starting digging up the same memories again, and I just lashed out. I only knew what I'd said years later, when people would come up to me and tell me how much I'd hurt them, like Derek or George Martin.

So when you sat down with David Sheff of Playboy *in 1980 …*
I didn't want to do that either, but Yoko threw the I-Ching, or that guy of hers read the tea leaves, or the Moon was in Capricorn or whatever she believed that week, and she said we had to do it. I mean, *Playboy*. Why would I want to be in that? It was a joke when we were kids. We'd look at the pictures to see what was going on, and it was all airbrushed and scrubbed. You couldn't see a thing. I always thought it was for fucking middle-aged business-men who couldn't get a hard-on.

Was Playboy *supposed to be an antidote to the* Rolling Stone *interview?*
No, we were just selling an album. It only became the 'last testament', or however

they sold it, after Chapman shot me, and I went into seclusion, or exile, like fucking Napoleon. Then Yoko negotiated a book deal – she was tougher than Klein or Epstein, or Geffen, any of them – and it became an event. She's good at those. Until then, it was just a guy following us round while we were making *Double Fantasy*. It got to be a pain. We'd nip out the back of the studio for a fag while they were reloading the tapes, and there would be David from *Playboy*, scared that he might be missing some pearl of wisdom from the Oracle.

Throughout that interview, you kept pushing the idea that you'd spent the previous five years as a house-husband, looking after Sean…
…And baking fucking bread. Don't remind me about it. We were selling a record, that's all it was. It was the first one for five years, and we knew that if we came out and said, look, we've been sat on our asses for five years, and we had a kid but he's being raised by the servants, and we've been on junk and hash and cocaine, and I couldn't write a fucking song to save my fucking life, that nobody would be interested.

So Yoko came up with this idea – the title, all that shit about the album being a heartsong, or a heartplay, and the whole PR bullshit about hanging up the guitar on the wall and spending five years as Father of the Year. Then when I get shot and I tell her that I'm not coming back, she starts going through the cupboards and digging up all these shitty tapes that prove exactly how empty and dried up and desperate I was during those five years. Now I don't have to try, and it's a great relief, I can tell you.

I used to feel ashamed sometimes, particularly when I saw Paul going through the same PR shit every time he put a record out. You could always tell when he was lying, because he tried too hard. But everyone always wanted to believe me. I had this reputation for telling it straight – honest John, shooting from the hip, and all that crap. But I was as big a bullshitter as any of them.

It was all to keep the myth alive, that fucking 'Ballad Of John And Yoko'. If I regret anything, it's writing that song. What was I fucking thinking of? "They're going to crucify me" – I might as well have put a contract on my own head. It was an invitation to the first maniac with a gun and a Beatles complex to come after me. And he did.

No sooner had you gone into seclusion in the early 80s than so-called 'insiders' started writing books about life with the Lennons at the Dakota. And they're still coming out. There were two books last year, by Geoffrey Guiliano and Robert Rosen, that were supposedly based on your diaries.

Which were stolen after the shooting, and some of them never fucking came back. Or I got photocopies maybe, I can't remember. Either way, those books are a joke. Look, I was lying to myself for years, and to the fans, and to Yoko. What makes you think that because I was secretly writing in a diary, I was telling myself the truth? You think I didn't realise that there would be professors and fucking students leafing through those books when I was dead, looking for another commandment from the fucking Holy Grail? I was cracking up when I wrote some of that stuff. It was like the books I wrote in the 60s, *In His Own Write* and the other one. I was just filling up time.

So when you wrote in your diaries about having erotic dreams about George Harrison or your mother ...

Give me more fucking taste than that, for God's sake, or Krishna's. George was a friend in the 60s when he was still a kid, and we took trips together and all that, and I know the Apple Scruffs all loved him, but you think I had nothing better than him to fantasise about? Anyway, he was too skinny for me. I always liked more meat on my bone, as they say in the Bronx.

I had to laugh when I read about the trial of the guy who stabbed George. I don't wish him, or anyone, any harm, and I was as shocked as the next guy when I saw it on TV. But what does he do when this madman comes at him with a knife? He starts singing the fucking Hare Krishna Mantra. I mean, it didn't even make No. 1 when he put it out on Apple. At least he could have sung one of his many hits. That would have scared the guy off.

Do you think any of those books came close to telling the truth about John Lennon?

Well, there is no truth, you know. There's only me, and that changes from day to day. I'm the only one who knows the truth, and I've read enough Freud, or Jung, or Janov, to know that I don't have any idea what's going on inside my head. I never did. So anyone who thinks they can pin me down by going through my diaries, or talking to Yoko's astrologer, or checking out my dry-cleaning, or even listening to my songs, you're fucking crazy. It's all an illusion. The more of that bullshit you believe, the further you get from the real me. Whoever he may be.

The only one of those books that I liked

was Albert Goldman. I liked his title, *The Lives Of John Lennon*. He realised that there was more than one. And he wasn't afraid to tell it straight. People hated him for it, saying that I beat people up, and tried to kill sailors, and fought with Stu Sutcliffe, and hit Sean, and took drugs – but it was all true. All my so-called nearest and dearest, the extended fucking Beatles family, were all outraged, but I was fucking thrilled. Because it took the pressure off.

I didn't have to hide the truth from anyone, or from myself. Goldman said I was a bastard, and I was violent, and I was weak, and he was right. That doesn't take away the songs, or the records, or Beatlemania, or whatever piece of my life you dissect for clues. It doesn't cancel out the Beatles, or the 60s, or any of those myths. But it's real. It says it the way it was. And if I was selling another record, which I won't be, I'd do it the same way. I'd tell the truth.

But you swore that you were telling the truth to Jann Wenner in 1970 and David Sheff in 1980. Why should we believe you now?

Because I've got nothing to sell. There's no need for bullshit, or newspaper taxis – which was Paul's line anyway, I'd like to point out. He can have it. He needs it more than me.

This is it. If you don't believe me, then you can fuck off, and go back to your Beatle books, and your Anthologies, and your old interviews. But they are all hype. We were just people, all of us, even Paul, and I'm the only one who is prepared to admit it. The others are going to have to keep walking round the wheel of karma, or whatever it turns out to be, until they realize it themselves. The whole world is still trapped in this fantasy of Beatlemania – everyone except me. It's a fucking joke, and I'm the only one smiling.

Stop Press: Books Arriving Too Late for Inclusion

Fargo Rock City: A Heavy Metal Odyssey in Rural North Dakota
By Chuck Klosterman £18.99 Hardback (700g) 288pp
Hilarious, young-man-growing-up-with-a-soundtrack, chronicle of Klosterman's formative years, combined with an unusual but compelling history of rock through the lens of '80s heavy metal. Original, off-beat and very funny.
  "If you love rock 'n' roll, you'll love *Fargo Rock City*." Stephen King

Ways of Hearing: A User's Guide to the Pop Psyche, from Elvis to Eminem
By Ben Thompson £14.99 Paperback (500g) 288pp
Taking a lead from John Berger's *Ways of Seeing*, Thompson rampages off on a frolic of his own, cutting through the flim flam, to gain access to the soul's inner ear. The cast of visionaries and pioneers includes Lee 'Scratch' Perry, Captain Beefheart, Lemmy, Chemical Brothers and The Pet Shop Boys.

Positively Fourth Street: The Lives and Times of Joan Baez, Bob Dylan, Mimi Baez Farina and Richard Farina
By David Hadju £16.99 Hardback (750g) 332pp
Beautifully written account of the central figures in the Greenwich Village scene, that also pushes the more contentious premise that ill-fated novelist Richard Farina virtually invented Bob's worldly-wise bohemian persona.

fa fa fa fa fa fa: The Adventures of Talking Heads
By David Bowman £16.99 Hardback (950g) 400pp
Novelist Bowman charts the history of one of rock's most intelligent bands from the dirty halls of CBGBs in 1976 on to a string of hits and a bitter break-up and aftermath. A fascinating story, very well told.
  Surely the wrong number of "fa"s though, sub-ed.

BIBLIOGRAPHY
AND ORDERING DETAILS

You Don't Know Me,
The Limits of Biography

Timeless Flight Revisited: The Definitive History of The Byrds – **Johnny Rogan £20.00 (2kg)** Extensively revised third edition of Rogan's fascinating saga of McGuinn, Hillman et al. 752 pages. 32 pages of photos The biggest ever biography of a rock band. New edition
  "The best biography of a beat group ever written by that most dedicated detective and interested observer; the caring, intelligent fan." Q

Dream Brother – **David Browne £17.99 HB 1857029887 (1kg)**
When Jeff Buckley drowned in 1997, the music world was shaken to its foundations, not least because of the echoes of his father Tim's demise. The book has been written with the full co-operation of Mary Guibert, Jeff's mother and Tim's first wife, and features interviews and extracts from Jeff's previously unpublished letters and diaries. One of the most eagerly anticipated music biographies in recent years. 384 pages plus photos

Behind The Shades: Take Two – **Clinton Heylin £20.00 HB 0670885061 (1.5kg)**

The first biography to adequately assess Dylan's life and work and work in the seventies and eighties: an essential piece of Dylanology, radically revised and completely updated to introduce Dylan as an artist for the new millennium. The most important book on Dylan to come out since Michael Gray's *Song and Dance Man*. 570 pages

Bob Dylan: Performing Artist Vol.1 1960-1973 – **Paul Williams £12.99 PB (600g)**

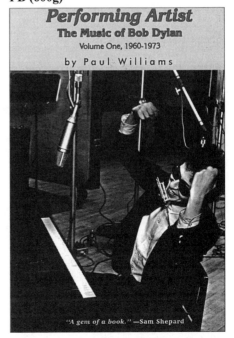

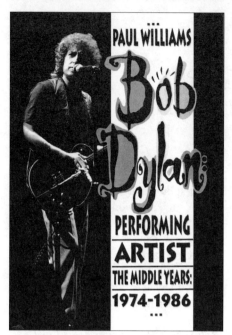

PAUL WILLIAMS
Bob Dylan
PERFORMING
ARTIST
THE MIDDLE YEARS:
1974-1986

Joel Selvin called *Performing Artist Volume 1* "The only Dylan book that matters". It was also enthusiastically received by the likes of Jerry Garcia, Sam Shepard and Allen Ginsberg.

***Bob Dylan Performing Artist Vol.2 1974-1986* – Paul Williams £12.99 PB 600g)**
"Williams remains the most eminently readable of all the Dylan commentators." *Record Collector*

***Down The Highway: The Life of Bob Dylan* – Howard Sounes £17.99 0385601255 HB**
Accessibly written and extraordinarily compelling, *Down the Highway* offers the most revelatory look ever at the public and private life of the man whose music has touched millions.

***Morrissey And Marr: The Severed Alliance* – Johnny Rogan £12.99 PB (650g)**
Authoritative study of the rise and fall, by the author of books on Neil Young and The Byrds, that was a huge critical and commercial success. Although one critic, SPM, wished Rogan a premature death in a M4 pile-up, this is how a group biography should be written. Highly recommended.

***Zero to Sixty* – Johnny Rogan £25.00 HB 0952954044 (1.5kg)**
The most authoritative and definitive study of Young's life and career yet written. This book tackles every phase of Young's life from his childhood in Canada until the end of the century with provocative commentaries from Neil, his friends, family, band members, producers and critics. 704 pages plus photos

Alan McGee and the Creation Myth

***The Creation Records Story : My Magpie Eyes Are Hungry for the Prize* – David Cavanagh £20.00 HB 1852277750 (1kg)**
The full story behind this maverick label which was the stable for many of the top indie bands in the eighties and nineties. Also provides a comprehensive overview of the indie scene of that era – perhaps the best book written on popular music written in 2000. 510 pages

***Story of Creation Records: This Ecstasy Romance Cannot Last* – Paolo Hewitt £9.99 PB 1840183500 (800g)**
Creation were one of *the* success stories of the nineties as Alan McGee's greatest discoveries, Oasis, swept all before them. Paolo Hewitt, with the full co-operation

of McGee, has written a blistering account of the label's history, taking in all the major signings, such as Primal Scream, House of Love, and Teenage Fanclub. 250 pages

We Think So You Don't Have To

Christagau's Albums of the 90s – **Robert Christagau £16.99 PB 0312245602 (1kg)**
The acclaimed rock critic collects brand new material and presents nearly 4,000 reviews on rap, country, blues, African, world music and rock. His grades (ranging from A+ to duds and turkeys) are universally accepted for building a strong collection. 544 pages

Mojo 1000 : the Albums That Define Popular Music – **edited by Jim Irvin £20.00 PB (1kg)**
A major release from the premier music magazine which utilises all the award-winning members of the writing team. This is an authoritative and engaging guide to the history of the pop album via hundreds of long-players, both the much-loved and the little-known.

(Virgin's) All Time Top 1,000 Albums – **edited by Colin Larkin £16.99 PB (650g)**
Unputdownable compendium of the great and the massive. From the usual Beatles and Dylanesque subjects, via 70s behemoths like Floyd and Zep to the new giants, Radiohead, Verve and Oasis.

A Whore Just Like All The Rest – **Richard Meltzer £12.50 PB (750g)**
Author of 'What a Goddam Great Second Cream Album', one of the first ever rock reviews ever written, Richard Meltzer has had a long and illustrious career in music

journalism. Amazingly, this is the first collection of his work, a remarkable document of an era by a singular voice in music writing.

A Singular Song

Dazzling Stranger: Bert Jansch And The British Folk And Blues Revival – **Colin Harper £25 HB**
The first authorised biography setting Bert Jansch in the wider context of the 1960s British Folk explosion. One of the best-ever books on a folk artist. 379 pages plus photos

McTell, Ralph Angel Laughter Autobiography Volume One – **Ralph McTell HB £15.00 (750g)**
First volume of the long-awaited autobiog of his early life as Ralph May, spanning

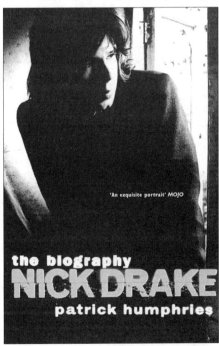

'An exquisite portrait' *MOJO*

the biography
NICK DRAKE
patrick humphries

the years from infancy in the late 1940s to his time in the Infantry Junior Leaders Battalion of the army at the age of 15. Told with grace and humour, this book gives the reader great insight into the early life of one of folk's great talents. 300 pages

Nick Drake – **Patrick Humphries £7.99 HB (400g)**
Massively influential (REM, Bragg, Eitzel, Weller) British songwriter who died at the tragic young age of 26 in 1974, gets the book he deserves by highly respected Richard Thompson biographer Humphries.

All Together Now?
The Beatles Anthology

The Beatles Anthology – **John Lennon, Paul McCartney, George Harrison, Ringo Starr £35.00 HB 0304356050 (2kg)**
This extraordinary book has been made possible because all three living Beatles and Yoko Ono Lennon have agreed to tell the full story at last – a painstaking compilation of sources world-wide ensures that John Lennon's words are equally represented. 367 pages

The Beatles: Off the Record, Outrageous Opinions and Unrehearsed Interviews – **Keith Badman, foreword by Hunter Davies £20.00 HB 0711979855 (1kg)**
Fresh from a considerable success with *The Beatles After The Break-Up*, Keith Badman has now produced the definitive book of quotes: from the Cavern days to the final split, here is the story of the Beatles in their own words, with comments from friends, associates and observers. A candid record

of the group as they were back then, that stands as an excellent companion to *The Anthology*, written from today's perspective. 600 pages plus photos

The Brian Epstein Story – **Debbie Geller £16.99 HB (1kg)**
The complex life of the most successful British rock manager was told in a BBC *Arena* documentary: this fascinating book draws on the dozens of interviews conducted for that programme and extracts from many of Epstein's personal diaries. One of the most important additions to Beatles scholarship in recent years. 288 pages, photos

Paul McCartney Many Years From Now – **Barry Miles £7.99 PB (500g)**
Miles and McCartney go back a long way as this excellent in-depth study shows. McCartney talks the reader through his life and music, song by song, and reminds us all that it was Macca who was the hip one for a while. This authorised biography is the nearest we're going to get to an autobiography. Essential reading for anyone with any interest whatsoever in The Beatles and the 60s.

Across The Great Divide.
Country And Rock

Are You Ready For The Country: Elvis, Dylan, Parsons And The Roots Of Country Rock – **Peter Doggett £8.99 PB (450g)**
Are You Ready For The Country tells the story of Country Rock. Utterly comprehensive, richly detailed, and packed full of the first-hand testimony of musicians, record executives, producers

and journalists, it is a superb guide to a uniquely American music and a very American state of mind.

***Desperados : The Roots of Country Rock* – John Einarson £13.99 PB (750g)**
The author of the best-selling biography on Buffalo Springfield takes a look at the mellow sound of Southern California, typified by groups like the Eagles and the Flying Burrito Brothers. 304 pages plus photos

Double Act

***Double Trouble : Bill Clinton and Elvis Presley in a Land of No Alternatives* – Greil Marcus £9.99 PB 0571204821 (800g)**
America's foremost rock critic revisits a favourite theme and displays typically angular thinking by bringing the Kid President into his thesis. As always, an erudite, funny and challenging read.

The Song Is Over

***Songwriters on Songwriting* – Paul Zollo £11.95 PB (600g)**
Interviews with the greatest practitioners. 500 pages

***Behind The Glass : Top Producers Tell How They Craft Their Hits* – Howard Massey £16.95 PB 0879306149 (750g)**
This book gives every musician and aspiring producer the secrets behind creating hit records and the inside story from the masters of the trade. Includes firsthand interviews with legendary producers as George Martin, Phil Ramone, Alan Parsons and Brian Wilson. 224 pages

'There's a kind of curve where you start from nothing, you learn the pieces and gradually get better and better until you reach a peak – then you start to go down. You need to catch the people at that peak.' – George Martin, from the book.

Le Jour De Gloire Est Arrivé L'Histoire De Serge Gainsbourg

***Serge Gainsbourg: View From the Exterior* – Alan Clayson £12.99 PB (500g)**
First English-language biography of the Gitanes-smoking French icon. 212 pages, b/w photos "A useful introduction to the man and his work." *Record Collector*

***Serge Gainsbourg: A Fistful of Gitanes* – Sylvie Simmons £12.99 PB (350g)**
Drawing on hours of new interviews with people Gainsbourg worked with, played with and loved, the author tells the story of the man who reinvented French pop and inspired a new generation of louche wannabes, and examines his rich musical legacy. 192 pages plus photos

Don Preston

***Necessity Is….: The Early Years of Frank Zappa & The Mothers Of Invention* Billy James £12.99 PB 0946719 144 (600g)**
Billy James has extensively interviewed original members of Frank Zappa's Mothers Of Invention – namely Bunk Gardner, Don Preston, Jimmy Carl Black, Ray Collins and Roy Estrada. Also includes info on other ex-members like Buzz Gardner, Lowell George, Art Tripp and Motorhead Sherwood. *Necessity Is...* perfectly captures and recreates the oddball humour that surrounded the Zappa entourage from 1964-1969. 192 pages, photos

OTHER RECENT AND FORTHCOMING TITLES OF INTEREST

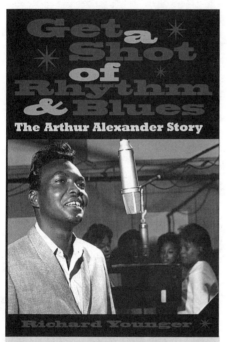

Get a Shot of Rhythm and Blues – the Arthur Alexander Story – **Richard Younger £17.50 PB 081731024x (650g)**
The first book-length biography of the influential soul/country legend whose songs have been recorded by the Beatles, the Rolling Stones and Dylan.

The Beach Boys: Pet Sounds by **Kingsley Abbott £12.00 1-900924-30-7 224 pages/ 8 pages b/w photos**

Kingsley Abbott draws on hours of new interviews to tell the full story of the album; from its composition and recording, through to its long-term legacy, as the greatest album popular music has yet produced. (Helter Skelter)

Eight Arms to Hold You – the Beatles Solo Compendium – **Chip Madinger and Mark Easter. £44.99 0615117244 PB 718pp**
Over thirty years in the making with twenty years research , the ultimate look at the solo careers of John Lennon, Paul McCartney, George Harrison and Ringo Starr, beyond the Beatles. Every aspect of their professional careers is explored: from recording sessions to TV and everything in between – all are exhaustively examined. (44.1 Productions, LP)

Jeff Beck: Crazy Fingers – **Annette Carson £10.99 0879306327 252pp**
The definitive biography of the reclusive, inventive guitarist who still pushes musical boundaries today. (Backbeat)

Rhythm Oil :A Journey Through the Music of the American South – **Stanley Booth. £11.95 0306809796 PB 254 pp**
As Booth makes his way from Memphis to the Mississippi Delta, to the depths of

the Georgia woods exploring the sounds, the music and the culture of the American South, "he has produced some of the most gracefully written , thoughtful and thought-stirring musings on the characters – the famous and the forgotten – who command the kingdom or drift through the shadowland of the South's rich patrimony." (Nick Tosches, *LA Times*)

The Big Book of the Blues: The Fully Revised and Updated Biographical Encyclopaedia – **Robert Santelli. £14.99 PB 0141001453**
With more than six-hundred entries, an indispensable blues reference work.

Blues Travelling : The Holy Site of Delta Blues – **Steve Cheseborough £14.99 PB 1578062322**
Almost as good as being there, this book takes you on a tour of the dusty roads and backwoods of Mississippi, the birthplaces, gravesites, churches and villages that gave birth to the blues.

Roy Buchanan: American Axe – **Phil Carson £14.99 0879306394 (750g)**
Buchanan melded blues, country, jazz and rock like no other guitarist, before or since. This is the bittersweet story of the 'guitarist's guitarist'.

I've Been Everywhere – A Johnny Cash Chronicle – **Peter Lewry £14.00 PB 1-900924-22-6 320pp**
Fully illustrated with many rare photos and other memorabilia, this is a complete account of his public life, including many rare and forgotten moments, all captured with the vibrant immediacy of diary entries. (Helter Skelter)

Only the Strong Survive – Memoirs of a Soul Survivor – **Jerry Butler, with Earl Smith £20.50 HB 0253337968**
Part-autobiography of one of the leading r-and-b and soul and part social history of the black music industry.

Callin' Out Around the World: A Motown Reader – **Kingsley Abbott £12.99 1-900924-14-5 256 pages, 8 pages of photos**
With a foreword by Martha Reeves, *Callin' Out Around The World* assembles a unique collection of articles on Motown's artists, musicians, writers and producers. Includes interviews with Berry Gordy, Martha Reeves, Marvin Gaye, The Miracles, The Supremes, *et al*; details of rare tracks; fresh new perspectives on Motown musicians and writers. Plus much, much more. (Helter Skelter)

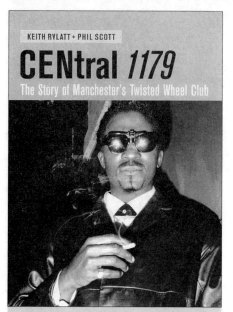

Central 1179: Manchester's Twisted Wheel Club – **Keith Rylatt and Phil Scott £19.95 09535662632 (1kg) PB**
The comprehensive and definitive history of the fabled Manchester Northern Soul club which closed in 1971. (Bee Cool)

This is Serbia Calling: Rock n Roll Radio and Belgrade's Underground Resistance – **Matthew Collin £9.99 1852426829 PB 245pp**
This is the story of B92, the independent Belgrade radio station and the courageous young people who ran it, waging a ten-year fight for freedom, armed only with a radio transmitter, some rock 'n' roll records and a dream of truth and justice. Despite police raids and censorship, they refused to be defeated. A unique insider's account of an epic cultural battle set in a world where rock 'n' roll ravers meet political activism, amid a climate of repression and ethnic cleansing. An inspiring read. (Serpents Tail)

The Song of Leonard Cohen – **Harry Rasky £13.50 0889637428 PB 160pp**.
Inspired by a recent conversation in which Cohen praised the film, *The Song of Leonard Cohen*, Rasky has created this powerful and moving text woven from his own archives and diaries. Also contains never-before-published Bob Dylan diaries, based on Rasky's notes from a documentary that was never completed. (Mosaic Press)

Bing Crosby: A Pocketful of Dreams, The Early Years 1903-1940 – **Gary Giddins. £24.99. 0316881880 HB 725pp**
Bing Crosby dominated American popular culture as no one else ever has, from Prohibition to Depression to World War II,

The Peacock Manifesto – **Stuart David £7.99 PB 09533 27558**
Join Glasgow's very own Rhinestone Cowboy, Peacock Johnson, in one of the best black comedies of the year.

he was the world's most beloved entertainer, and much more. A musical innovator, he practically invented modern pop singing bringing a dramatic intimacy to records, radio and movies. This definitive biography rescues Crosby from mythographers and debunkers alike, drawing on hundreds of interviews and unprecedented access to numerous archives, Gary Giddins dramatises the ascension of pop and reclaims Crosby's central role in American cultural history. (Little, Brown)

Making Of Kind of Blue – **Ashley Khan £20.00 HB 1862074240 (1kg)**
An essential accompaniment to a modern classic, exploring the careers and

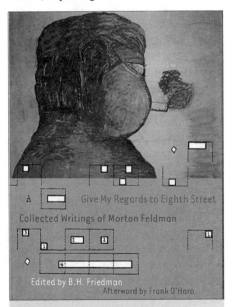

Give My Regards to Eighth Street – Collected Writings of Morton Feldman – **ed. B.H. Friedman. £9.95 PB 1878972316**
Funny and illuminating, the collected musings of one of the most influential American composers of the 20th century.

struggles of all the musicians involved. Ashley Khan has listened to all the tapes and interviewed all the survivors.

Miles Beyond: The Electric Explorations of Miles Davis 1967-1991 – **Paul Tingen £20.50 PB 0823083462**
An in-depth exploration of Davis' controversial electric period and the impact it had on the jazz world.

Back Pages: The Definitive Bob Dylan Encyclopaedia – **Oliver Trager £13.50 PB 0684857413**
The A-Z of all things Dylanological; life events, songs, reviews etc

Living with Music: Ralph Ellison's Jazz Writings – **ed. Robert O'Meally £16.99 PB 0679640347**
Examines the lesser-known musical life of Ellison, as seen through his fictional and non-fictional essays, including profiles of the jazz greats.

Stan Getz: An Appreciation of His Recorded Work – **Ron Kirkpatrick £4.99 0952010704 PB 48pp**
A chronological analysis of Getz's recorded works interspersed with biographical details. Listing all musical collaborators and dates/venues of recordings, Kirkpatrick discusses the most representative of the recordings which have been published on cd. An informative and insightful book of thoughtful criticism. (Zany publications)

Strange Fruit: The Biography of a Song – **David Margolick £9.99 0060959568**
The extraordinary voice of Billie Holiday transformed this song into an agonising indictment of racial prejudice in the USA.

1000 Great Guitarists – **Hugh Gregory £9.99 PB 1871547741**
Guitar heroes from every genre imaginable.

Janis Joplin: Scars of Sweet Paradise – **Alice Echols £8.99 1860499031 PB (800g)**
A major biography of one of the most distinctive female voices in the history of rock, with contributions from many of her friends and collaborators, revealing an artist who was loved and loathed in equal measure. (Little, Brown)

Jazz – A History of America's Music – **Geoffrey C. Ward and Ken Burns £30.00 0712667695 PB 488pp**
The book of the BBC series. A detailed history of jazz bound up with the story of race in America, two world wars, drugs and the Depression era. Above all it is the story of dozens of extraordinary musicians. In this powerful narrative, Ward and Burns bring to life the men and women whose legacies have left a lasting imprint on our culture. From Benny Goodman to Ornette Coleman, Ella Fitzgerald and Billie Holiday to name just a few, this magnificently illustrated book puts the evolution of jazz into a cultural context. Marvellously readable. There is simply no other book on jazz like it. (Pimlico)

Sun Prints – **Linda McCartney £24.99 0821227378 PB**
Paul McCartney has written the introduction to this collection of his late wife's photographic portraits, landscapes and still-lifes. A gifted photographer, this book highlights Linda's inspired experiments with the nineteenth-century sun printing technique.

Blackbird Singing: Poems and Lyrics 1965-1999 **Paul McCartney £14.99 057120789 HB 164pp**
The poet, Adrian Mitchell, writes in his introduction "Clean out your head. Wash out the name and the fame. Read the clear words and listen to them – decide for yourself. Paul is not in the line of academic poets or modernist poets. He is a popular poet". (Faber and Faber)

Nothing – **Paul Morley. £11.99 0571177999 PB 426pp**
"I remember that my father killed himself. I suppose that means I must have a good memory". In typically idiosyncratic fashion, Morley reveals the past he has long struggled to forget: his childhood in Stockport, teenage years and the unfathomable suicide of his depressive father. A funny and engaging work of confession.

God, Guns and Rock n Roll – **Ted Nugent. £20.50 0895262797 HB 315pp**
Enter the world of Ted Nugent – rock 'n'

roll star, marksman, hunting advocate, anti-drugs campaigner. As Ted says, "You either believe in the Constitution and the Ten Commandments or you've got a problem."

Gram Parsons: God's Own Singer – **Jason Walker £12.99 PB 1-900924-277**
Jason Walker has conducted hundreds of hours of new interviews with Gram's fellow musicians, friends and associates to paint a vivid portrait of the beautiful, doomed Southern rich kid who brought Nashville to rock 'n' roll. (Helter Skelter) 256 pages, 8 pages of photos

The Faber Companion to Twentieth Century Popular Music – **Phil Hardy £20 PB 05719608x·**
An indispensable reference work – everything and everyone from Abba to ZZ Top.

The King on the Road: Elvis Live on Tour 1954 to 1977 – **Robert Gordon. £22.95. 0312273215 PB**
This remarkable collection of never-before-published photos, posters, news reports and even ticket stubs adds up to a lavishly illustrated, definitive record of Elvis' on-stage career. 208pp. 300 colour and b-and-w photos.

The Shadows at EMI – the Vinyl Legacy – **Malcolm Campbell £15.00 0953556719 PB (750g)**
An exhaustively researched volume focusing on material recorded for EMI both in their own right and with Cliff Richard.

The True Adventures of the Rolling Stones – **Stanley Booth £13.99 PB 1556524005**
No less an authority than Keith Richards has recommended this book. We need say no more.

Old Gods Almost Dead: The 40-Year Odyssey of the Rolling Stones – **Stephen Davis £22.50 PB 0767903129 (1kg)**
With more than 20 previously unpublished photos, this is a complete history of the Stones.

Sonny Rollins: The Man and His Music – **Peter Niklas Wilson £15.95 1893163067 PB 256pp (750g)**
Wilson's biography of Rollins presents the life and legend of one of the most remarkable players and personalities in jazz. The book provides an in-depth analysis of key aspects of Rollins' music and his eccentric repertoire. An annotated and illustrated discography surveys the nearly 100 albums he has recorded throughout his lengthy career. 136 photos.

FIRE & RAIN
The James Taylor Story

Ian Halperin

Fire and Rain : The James Taylor Story – **Ian Halperin £9.99 PB 1840184345 (600g)**
Remarkably, the first-ever biography of one of the great singer-songwriters, his eventful life, many loves and songs.

Society Blues – **Elijah Wald. £24.99 1558492690 HB 336 pp (750g)**
A gifted and charismatic entertainer, Josh White (1914-1969) was a blues star of the '30s, cabaret star of the '40s, and a folk star of the '50s and '60s. In 1963 Billboard magazine ranked him America's third most popular folk singer, surpassed only by Pete Seeger and Harry Belafonte, and ahead of Bob Dylan. Elijah Wood traces White's journey from childhood, leading blind singers in Greenville, South Carolina, to the heights of Manhattan café society, explaining his struggles with discrimination, his political involvements and sometimes raucous personal life. "The best book on American music I've read in years" (Dave van Ronk). (University of Massachusetts Press)

Dumb Angel: The Life and Music of Dennis Wilson – **Adam Webb £11.95 1840680512 (500g)**
With a foreword written by Peter Buck of REM, this book details the musical gift – and tragic end – of the most soulful Beach Boy.

Jackie Wilson – The Man, the Music and the Mob – **Tony Douglas £15.99 1840184132 HB (850g)**

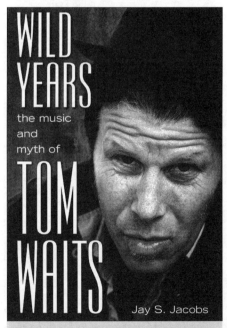

WILD YEARS
the music and myth of
TOM WAITS

Jay S. Jacobs

Wild Years: The Music and Myth of Tom Waits – **Jay S. Jacobs £16.99 PB 155022414x (500g)**
The first detailed biography of one of music's great eccentric talents.

Written with the co-operation of Wilson's family, lovers and friends, this book is a remarkable account of the musical genius and human tragedy that was Jackie Wilson's life. (Mainstream)

***In A Silent Way–A Portrait of Joe Zawinul* – Brian Glasser £15.00 1860743269 HB 335pp (750g)**
Joe Zawinul is the most important European in the history of jazz. With his group, Weather Report, he pioneered the last seismic shift American jazz has known – the incorporation of world music rhythms and new electronic tonalities, loosely known as fusion – and they enjoyed more than 15 years of success. This book tells Joe's remarkable story in depth. Includes original interviews with Zawinul himself, collaborators, and friends – from Thelonious Monk to the president of Austria! – from the 1940s to the present day. (Sanctuary)

WAYS OF HEARING

A user's guide to the pop psyche, from Elvis to Eminem

BEN THOMPSON

***Ways of Hearing* – Ben Thompson £14.99 PB 0575068094 (600g)**
Part Pop Hall of Fame, part self-help manual, and part-visionary manifesto.

How to order

Please order by title, author and price. Always quote your post code (UK). Orders can be made either by post, fax, email or telephone.

Finally, when placing an order, please give a telephone number so that out of stock titles can be notified immediately.

How to pay

Payment must be received with the order.

UK: by cheque [payable to Helter Skelter Limited], postal order, Mastercard or Visa.

If ordering by credit card, please include the following: type of credit card, cardholder's name, cardholder's full address, card number and expiry date.

Overseas: by International Money Order, Bank draft [drawn on a UK bank] Credit card [details required as above, sterling cash sent registered.

Please do not send foreign currency, or cheques drawn on overseas banks.

Postage charges

Please add together the weights shown against each book, match the total with the chart below to calculate the cost of the postal charges for your order.

Weight not over	UK& Channel islands**	EIRE (air)	Europe (air)	USA, Canada & Rest of World excl *** (air)	***Australasia and Far East (air)	Overseas (Surface)
250g	£1.00	£1.50	£1.50	£3.50	£4.00	£1.50
500g	£1.50	£2.00	£2.00	£5.00	£6.00	£2.50
750g	£2.50	£3.00	£3.00	£7.00	£8.50	£3.00
1kg	£3.50	£4.00	£4.00	£9.00	£10.50	£4.00
2kg	£4.00	£8.00	£8.00	£17.00	£20.00	£7.50
3kg	£4.75	£12.00	£12.00	£25.00	£30.00	£10.50
4kg	£4.75	£16.00	£16.00	£33.00	£40.00	£14.00
5kg*	£4.75	£20.00	£20.00	£41.00	£45.00	£17.00

All UK Consignments from 5kg to 30kg will cost £4.50
250g, 500g & 750g rates for the UK are for second class postage.
1kg rate is for 1st class.
For parcels greater than 5kg overseas, please telephone for postage charges
All parcels to Europe are sent by air.
ALL IN-STOCK ITEMS DESPATCHED WITHIN 48 HOURS
**From time to time lower UK postage rates will be advertised at a lower
rate, in which case these rates will supersede this table

Business hours Mon-Fri 10.00-7.00, Sat 10.00-6.00
the phone may take longer than usual to be answered between 5.00 and 5.15 as that is
when we stop for afternoon tea and cakes

Helter Skelter Limited
4 Denmark Street, London WC2H 8LL United Kingdom
Tel 44 (0) 20 7836 1151 Fax 44 (0) 20 7240 9880 email helter@skelter.demon.co.uk
website http://www.skelter.demon.co.uk